IN THE MIDDLE

New Writing from the Midlands

First published 2020 by Dahlia Publishing Ltd
6 Samphire Close Hamilton
Leicester LE5 1RW
ISBN 9781913624019

LOTTERY FUNDED

Supported using public funding by

ARTS COUNCIL
ENGLAND

CONTENTS

About Middle Way Mentoring

The Middle Way Mentoring Programme is a two year professional development scheme for Black, Asian, Minority Ethnic writers based in the Midlands.

Writers received mentoring for a period of twelve months from an experienced writer, and participated in a series of masterclasses designed to develop the craft of writing. Mentors included Susmita Bhattacharya, Rebecca Burns, Rod Duncan, Lily Dunn, Tania Hershman, Mahsuda Snaith, and Kerry Young.

During the second year, writers participated in a series of workshops and talks delivered by industry experts, received bespoke career coaching. They also began to focus on completing a portfolio of short stories to send out to prizes, literary journals and to put forward for the scheme's anthology.

The Middle Way Mentoring project is led by writer and publisher, Farhana Shaikh with the support of a number of partners, including University of Leicester, CAMEo, Writing East Midlands, Writing West Midlands, Dahlia Publishing and Renaissance One, and funded by Arts Council England.

JIGNESH VAIDYA was born in Mumbai in September 1970. When I was two years old I contracted polio and have been paralysed in both my legs ever since. Due to my disability, I did not therefore have much schooling in India. By the time I was sixteen my family relocated to Dubai with my father's work where we lived for around two years. In December 1988 my family came to England. Due to my father's work for the British Bank, I was born a British Citizen, but first arriving in London at age eighteen, I did not speak a word of English and had never been to school.

Once living in Leicester I was able to go to college where I was taught to speak, read and write in English. Eventually, I began to work at local council as a volunteer, and finally found a paid job aged twenty eight with the BBC local radio. I began to realise how my life story interested people and was asked by various charities and organisations to help promote disability awareness. From this, I came to gain more confidence in writing in English as I understood that I had an important message to tell. Inspired by this, and by the impact, I realised my favourite sport, wheelchair basketball, could have on the confidence and lifestyle of disabled athletes, I put lots of work into promoting positive messages of disability sport.

The Boy in the Hole tells my unique journey from a difficult childhood in India, through my journey across half-the-world, to fight for equality, independence and success in my current life in United Kingdom. Charting my remarkable experiences across continents and different languages, my story shows my fight and determination to achieve equality in disability.

I wrote *The Boy in the Hole* after being encouraged by the motivational speeches I presented to students. At first they didn't believe that despite having contracted polio at two years old in India which stopped me walking, and not having a wheelchair until I was fourteen, that I had learnt to speak English at twenty and found a successful career in England, despite limited access to education. Finding my first paid job in my late twenties and learning to drive, the charity Scope suggested that I record my story in the hope to inspire those like me to stay positive in their journey whatever barriers we face.

Jignesh was mentored by Lily Dunn.

The Boy in the Hole

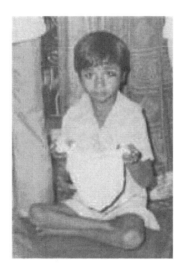

The sun beat down from the cloudless sky on my tiny head, my body submerged in the sand, that isolated insignificant head of a young child with only a crop of dark curly hair as a barrier between him and the relentless sun. I remember how the sun made me dizzy. I could lay my ear down on the hot earth next to me to rest it. I watched the children, among them my older brother and two sisters, running and playing, and I believed it - because my mother, Maa I called her, told me so earnestly - that if I stood submerged in the sandy earth of the hole all day, the gods would see me. Standing upright in the ground would heal me. Then one day I would run with the other children, rather than longingly watch them from my hole; one day when my legs would work again.

I was born in Mumbai on September 13th, 1970. It was a city of eclectic Persian architecture, ragged markets richly perfumed with intoxicating scents and spices, and ramshackle slum housing in foundations of mud. Kandiwali, south of Mumbai, a town of steel and fabric merchants. My family spanned four generations of village doctors – I was the youngest of four siblings – and we lived in an affluent home. We were comfortable and well respected back then.

The first home I actually remember was vastly different. It was in Ghakatoper, only a few miles walk, but a world away from my birth house. It was sparse and derelict. The changed came from a simple drink of water. In India – indeed still in England at that time – immunisation from polio was still being developed. My parents had paid for my older siblings, my brother and sisters, to have the injections, and it was intended that I be immunised, too. But, most likely from water, I contracted polio.

My first memory is not of home, but of hospital. A rundown building with a long corridor and high up windows I was too small to see through. From behind them jarred the noise of impatient traffic with piercing horns. For a two-year-old there was nothing but a confusing vast space teaming with urgent nurses and screaming children, their desperate parents asking 'what is wrong with my child?' I lay terrified and confused, wrapped head to toe in bandages like a mummy. So hot in the blistering Indian heat, and yet I was swaddled, unable to move and explore. The terrifying pain of needles and stitches, the horror at seeing a doctor come to my bed and all that my young mind had learnt to associate with him. Now, nearly fifty years later, the pearly white scars on my legs and arms remain to take me back to those painful moments from long ago.

My clearest memory is of a single face, full of hope and dreams for my recovery, my mother Nirmala. She was delicate and petite, her long dark hair fell long below her shoulders in waves, her golden bangles jangled as she reached out to hold me. Whatever horrors she was having to watch me endure, she calmly sat by my bed and held my hand. She was determined to do whatever it took to get me the right help and treatment. In Gujarati Maa means mother. She was my sole comfort and I knew that no matter what was happening, whilst she was there I would be safe. When she smiled with tears glittering in her eyes, she helped me know it would somehow be alright.

But whatever the hospital was doing, it didn't work. My legs were paralysed. The polio remained, and it was six months before I was allowed to go home. I spent those six months staring at the ceiling, thinking every day there would be a change, my legs would begin to work and I'd be discharged. I longed to go home. I remembered the Indian music from films that Maa would play on the radio as she cooked. I longed to sit in her arms and listen to her sing as

I went to sleep. There was no quiet for music in the hospital: the sound of crying children and hospital trolleys would drown it out. Finally discharged because there was nothing more the hospital could do to heal me, and it was not to the same house – we had been banished to a shanty town.

Some people, who believe in myths, say those who are disabled are cursed, punished by the gods. Disability is a mark that you have sinned in a past life. Some say that god is in the holy form of a sacred cow, or an elephant. If a cow is in front of us on the dusty street we must move for it, we must respect the cow out of reverence for god. Some adorn statues of cows or elephants in gold and haars, which are reefs of flowers, which will bring good fortune. I remember watching the people move aside for the reverent cow. I remember how the people scorned me, a child punished by the gods, punished with polio. And I began to understand deep down, that my family only lived as they did now, in poverty and shame, because my parents, Baap and Maa, had chosen *me*. Members of my own family believed I was a mark of shame to them.

After I had been released from hospital I remained in plaster for a few more following years; the solid white plaster running down each of my legs. Every other week we returned to the hospital for physiotherapy appointments where I was given hot oil massages on both my legs where my legs were stretched, my toes were pulled, and the sole of my feet were vigorously rubbed. Then I had my new plaster fitted for the following fortnight. Although many in my family and community would put more trust in 'mambo jambo', Maa, caring for me on her own now, kept believing that the hospital was my best help. For these appointments she determinedly carried me across Mumbai on two buses as we couldn't afford a taxi. Maa had to fight her way through the crowds, which would clear for a cow yet not for a struggling young mother with a child solid in plaster. As we boarded and exited the buses, our fellow travellers would stare at us in scorn without any offer of help. I see Maa in my mind, struggling to carry me in her arms, and I was helpless there and trusting that with her I was safe, yet knowing that no help, not even a kind word, would come our way.

Maa took that fortnightly journey for me as I grew, it becoming more and more evident to the by-passers who watched us with derision, that here was a boy whose legs didn't work, a boy the gods had marked in punishment, a boy who carried evil. She made this journey every fortnight from when I was three, until I was eleven, carrying me in her arms. All those early physiotherapy appointments, against tradition, against religion, she took me to without fail. She'd had everything when married at twenty, all provision. Maa's marriage had been arranged by her family who had chosen a man of good family standing who could promise her a comfortable life in which she was well provided for. He bestowed upon her a traditional wealth of heavy golden jewellery: necklaces, earrings, bracelets – I was so familiar with the weight of them on my fragile arms. All those promises, and that promised life, had been lost to her because of me. She now worked in a local factory constructing food machinery.

Many people in Mumbai still viewed modern medicine – the likes of physiotherapy – with suspicion. People in the villages believed that the leaves from certain trees were medicine, more trusted than any new-fangled hospital. Maa was strongly coerced by family and friends with knowledge of the sacred traditions of a thousand years that I might be able to walk again if I followed the practices of ancient Indian medicine. She must have clung to this hope, and that we might be accepted back to Kandiwali where I had been born. So she placed me in a hole.

Outside our house, family friends dug the hole, about 5ft under, and then in I went. My legs first, straight down in a standing position, earth buried to my neck. I was out in the hole every day, all day, allowed only water, with the sun of over 30 degrees blazing down onto my solitary head. When I came out I had to sit on the wall with heavy metals bangles hung on both of my fragile suffering legs.

Once back in the thankful shade of the house for the evening I put on my calliper, a walking frame, to do my exercises. I had to 'walk' from one and of the of the cobbled dusty courtyard from outside my house to the end of the yard, 10 doors down. The calliper was strapped to my legs and I had to move my legs using the sticks under my arms to operate it, the strain mostly going into my back and upper arms, whilst my knees ached. I had to do these exercises for twelve rounds. It was a cruel reward to be out of the hole and forced into walking with pain in every enforced step. Back in the house in the evening Maa would lastly massage my legs with hot oil, something I could mercifully look forward to as it was so peaceful and relaxing in contrast to the pain and frustration of the exercises. But my legs still did not work.

For a number of years this relentless practice continued day after day. I cried, but I knew in the hole that no one would wipe my tears. Maa had to work at the factory and my sisters were at school. People kept telling me it was for my own good, that one day I could walk again. From my hole I watched children playing cricket, going to school, doing normal things a child my age should do. They ran to catch the cricket ball. They ran back and forth from the cricket stumps. They played skipping with long coiled ropes. As I watched, a head in the dust, a little boy in a standing position, who otherwise could not stand. I found I could wriggle so slightly my big left toe, and slightly my smaller toes on the right. I delighted in that, feeling the tiny movement in the cool earth, wondering what would it be like when one day I would move all my toes, my whole foot at the ankle, my knees, my legs.

Other treatment that tradition swore by was to purify my diet. Someone wise must have told my parents that if I didn't eat any salt then I would improve faster, and would of course walk one day. To have no salt was the toughest constraint as salt was on everything! For a very long time I was allowed to eat only *bath* and *dahee* which was rice and yogurt.

In our small Chali society we had a lady who came to do peoples' laundry and cleaning. Her name was Saventabai. For her services Saventabai was paid in food which she stored in a cupboard in our house. As I was always so hungry and weak from my no salt diet, I craved the scent of food I saw placed in that cupboard. The temptation was so great that whilst Saventabai hung the washing outside, I became an afternoon thief. I secretly taught myself to shuffle on my bottom, pushing myself with my arms and hands for small distances from one place to another to retrieve any hidden food when no one suspected I could do anything but sit. I was a thief for more than a month, every day taking one or two *chapatti*, *saag*, *dal* and *jalebi*. Of course, one day I was inevitably caught by Saventabai who noticed her food was disappearing. She knew she had to tell Maa, who at first didn't believe her as she couldn't understand how I could possibly have moved to get it. Neither of them told anyone. Instead Maa decided that my no salt diet was useless. She told Baap that it was making me weak and miserable, and that the food full of salt I had secretly been eating did me no harm. Yet at first Baap said 'no.' After lots of conversations and Maa pleading for me to be allowed to eat properly, Baap eventually relented and I was allowed to eat like my brother and sisters. Not long after that, Baap left for Dubai.

Over a decade later Baap came home to tell us that we were leaving India. He had visited us on short trips here and there over the years but now we were travelling with him to Dubai. I understood he had been working for BBME (British Bank of the Middle East). He had secured us an apartment in a place called Jbara. Once there I found Dubai depressing, as despite the excitement of moving to a new country, I was still housebound. Sometimes Baap would hire a taxi in the evening when he returned from work and take me for a ride around Dubai. I remember seeing the bright lights and the busy streets, and we would stop to buy kabbous, a spicy vegetable wrap.

People kept advising Baap and Maa to go to the UK. I learnt that from 1963 they had been British citizens due to his work for BBME as a clerk. He had started the job in Yemen a year after they married, then returning to Mumbai in 1968 after being transferred with the bank. As a hard worker he had started as a runner for different banks since leaving school in the late 1950s. Eventually his hard work paid off and he ended up as Head of Administration before he retired late in 1995.

Looking into the possibility of moving to England, my brother Nisith, who was 23 by then, went ahead to London. It was Christmas Day, in freezing 1988 where our PIA (Pakistan International Airline) flight landed on Christmas Day morning. I was eighteen. I had never heard of Christmas before, but I remember seeing decorated trees at the airport, which was curious, but not as puzzling as seeing so many white non-Asian people. I watched my dad having a conversation at the immigration desk, but didn't understand what he was saying: I'd never heard him speak English before.

I found out later that there had been a problem. My sister Jagruti and I were now over 18, and yet our names were still on our mother's passport. I still remember Mr J Singh, informing Baap in a strange language and Baap shouting desperately back in words I didn't understand. But I guessed Mr Singh was telling us that he couldn't let us into UK. Baap pleaded him over and over, saying that due to my disability we couldn't get hold of separate passports in Dubai. As we were British citizens where else should we go? All five of us were sent to wait in an office for over two hours. We didn't know what would happen. We didn't have anywhere to go back to. Dubai was not our country, it seemed neither was India now...

We were sent to a small bland office, the walls painted stark white with a framed map of Britain handing on the wall alongside a portrait painting of the Queen of England (who could possibly guess I would actually meet her twenty-five years when invited me to her Buckingham Palace garden party). The room was too small to fit Maa, Baap, myself and two sisters with a bulky mahogany desk and only two chairs for us to sit on. A few hours later a white immigration officer D. Garfield, dressed in a dark suit and tie came in with Mr Singh, who wore a similar suit but with a navy blue turban. The stood at the other side of the polished desk to us. Baap was so nervous, All three talked in fluent English, and kept looking back at me. Finally they shook hands and the immigration officers left us in the office. Baap had convinced them. Mum had tears in her eyes, and I sat right next to her, with my sisters beside me. After a couple of deep breaths Baap told us how Mr Garfield was going to stamp our passports and we would pass customer services and we were reunited with our my older brother. Baap later told us Mr Garfield was a very nice and understanding immigration officer just like Mr Singh. They understood why we, my sister and me, still had our names only on Maa's passport. If we had tried to apply for new passports in Dubai once we had turned eighteen it was likely that we would only have been authorised with Indian passports whilst the rest of the family held British. Mr Garfield allowed us entry as long we obtained new passports before our next birthday.

Finally seeing my brother again at the airport arrivals brought me such a big smile and tears in my eyes. I hadn't seen Nisith in over three years and I remember him hugging me and carrying me just like Maa used to when we were back in India. He took us to the car park where his boss waiting for us with his van to take to us Leicester, our new home. He had rented us a smart Victorian townhouse just off what would eventually become known as the Golden Mile. I was astounded at our new house which had seven rooms and a long hallway and landing and a paved courtyard

13

garden flanked by a high red brick wall. In the sitting room we sat around the gas fire which we lit with matches and shivered incessantly because it was so cold.

I had only ever had use of a wheelchair for a single year in Mumbai, and when we left for Dubai I could not take it with me. For the first few months in Leicester I waited for my assessment for a wheelchair. For these initial months I remember how I used to sit on the window sill and look at the world going by, thinking how very different life looked through a window in cold grey England, wondering curiously at the fallen white snow and the children throwing snow balls. I asked Maa to bring a handful inside for me to touch. I wondered at the houses along the street which had actual trees in their windows sprinkled with lights and garish tinsel, and why once the snow was melted the trees disappeared too when it had all been so beautiful.

When I think back to my early memories like these, I know now why, in England, I enjoy eating out and tasting food from all countries of the world, although jappattis, jalebi and saag curiously remain my favourite! I know why I love playing sport in my wheelchair, because of the freedom I never thought I'd have, chasing after the ball like I never thought I could. I know from my childhood why spending so many years in a hole gave me the restlessness to yearn to travel, and there is nothing I enjoy more than flying all over the world from New York and around Europe, Thailand and Turkey, Australia, and planning a safari trip to South Africa for my fiftieth birthday in a few years' time. I know why I always challenge myself, to do skydiving, to ride an elephant in Phuket, or a camel in Morocco, or swim in an ancient Roman pool in the mountains of Pamukkale, and drive a hand controlled car from Scotland to London, savouring when strangers in a car park see me in a chair and ask me how I can possibly drive? I know every time how much a simple act of kindness, the simple holding open of a door with a smile, whilst to most in England is a basic second-nature, to me I don't think anyone could know how much that means to me. And I know also from those memories why I can do all these things, because Maa always believed that somehow I could be healed, that somehow everything would be alright one day and I would be able to 'walk' again. If only Maa could have known back in Mumbai that whether I could be healed to walk again or not, I would be alright regardless. She was always there through it all, fighting against tradition to get the best for me. When I remember the boy in the hole, I don't think anyone would have suspected how far one day he would travel, how far he would fly, and how much one day he could do.

SARAH M JASAT grew up believing her family was very strange but later discovered she was Indian. Since she took part in the Becoming a Writer course she has focused on short fiction and has been published in Reflex Fiction, Bandit Fiction, Electric Town Lit and Lockdown Baby Babble. She dreams of writing a longer novel for older children if only she could get her own child to go to sleep.

What is family? What are the limits and the rules? How does it affect the way we relate to one another? Growing up in a tiny family, I was naive to family complexities until getting married. When I've encountered situations that confuse me, I have tried to explore them in fiction.

My short fiction explores how individuals struggle within constraints dictated by tradition and custom, in three wildly different pieces, using both traditional storytelling and more experimental forms. 'Rex Is Not The Name Of The Hamster You Had When You Were Six' shows a child unable to mourn and the effect it has on the rest of his life. 'Three Bedrooms, Completely Detached' sees a mother-in-law grieve the loss of her daughter-in-law, when her son's marriage breaks down. 'The One Where She Wanted To Break Things' looks at how a modern couple struggle in a traditional household.

Sarah was mentored by Tania Hershman.

Rex is Not The Name Of The Hamster You Had When You Were Eight

You do not want to touch the body.

You say so as clearly as you can. It's not difficult. There are no tricky sounds. No 'r's or worse, the 'shh' sound that your speech therapist spent an hour of last week's session trying to coax out of you. You say the words properly, you think, but everyone is still looking at you, so you say it again.

Your younger brother Rajah has no such reservations. He is crouched next to the long metal box that you do not want to look at. Rajah can crouch with his feet flat on the ground. You've tried but you can't, even though you're the older brother.

'Cold,' he says.

You can't believe him for sure though, because everyone says he is very young. Rajah is too young to really understand. Rajah is too young to remember.

You are four years older than Rajah.

'I know this is tricky for you.' Daddy kneels in front of you. You hear that word a lot these days. Your speech therapist and your teachers and your Daddy all use it. Even the word is tricky for you. 'tr' is almost as bad as 'shh'.

Last month it was your birthday and your parents gave you a golden hamster. His name is Jonas, or maybe Rex. You're not sure, though Jonas is easier for you to say. You've asked for a pet for years, since the neighbours got a

17

spotted Labrador that they sometimes let you walk around the block. Jonas is nice but you hope if you take good care of him you can get a dog next year.

You think about Jonas and don't look at the box.

'Don't force him,' someone says. Daddy sighs and stands up.

'Go and play then,' he says.

You go upstairs, take Jonas out of his cage and hold his warm body in your two hands, feel the heat through his golden fur. The next week Jonas is renamed Freddy, and months later turns still overnight, without warning. This too you do not touch, and when Daddy asks if you would like a dog, you shake your head. Rajah grows up, grows past you, marries a quiet girl who brings you food in Tupperware boxes each weekend, and talks about you in hushed tones on the phone to her relatives. You dote on your nieces and nephews, visiting new-borns in the hospital and gifting older ones with sweets and toys, but never pets. You turn 43, still four years older than Rajah, now one year older than Mummy. You wonder what might have happened, what your life might have been like, if Daddy had asked one more time.

3 Bedrooms, Completely Detached

Thank you *so* much for coming over. Please, come inside. Are you the lady I spoke to on the phone yesterday? Like I was saying, I wanted to get started right away, now that I've made the decision, so it's just so kind of you to fit me in.

If you're ready, shall I take you around?

This is the kitchen. It's a good place to start, isn't it? I've always felt it's the real heart of the home so we extended it right away and it's a good size for a family. Such a lovely feeling when you're cooking together--

Excuse me, I'm just getting over a cold. Nothing to worry about. While we're here would you like a cup of tea or maybe something to eat? Oh, but the milk– I'll just check, I think it's curdled. I'll throw it out. There were biscuits somewhere. This cupboard? Or here. Just some water then? I'm so sorry, I haven't managed to go shopping. I'll get you a clean glass from the cupboard.

Here's the lounge – we broke through the wall to combine the two rooms. We wanted more space when we started a family. There used to be toys everywhere, under the sofa, behind the television. That was a different time – my son, he's grown up now.

The hallway, I suppose it has become dated... You don't notice as the years go by, do you? We did it all up when we moved in, but that was... let's see... over twenty years ago. I'm sure the new owners will want to redecorate to their tastes. They'll probably change everything. Yes, I understand that we'll have to allow for that in the price.

Did you hear a knock at the door just then? I thought I heard— Sometimes the doorbell doesn't work, you see, and I wouldn't want anyone to be waiting. I'll just check quickly, won't be a moment.

Oh. No one there.

Nevermind.

Where was I? These are the original stairs. We did once look at getting them changed. We thought the wood was a bit old fashioned and one of the neighbours had got a modern glass and steel staircase fitted, but then we thought for grandchildren it's not practical is it? They'll cover the glass in finger marks and goodness knows what else. Oh no, no, no, we don't have any grandchildren at the moment. It's just what we were thinking at the time. It's not in our hands, is it?

Upstairs hallway. There are three bedrooms. Always a bit more than we needed. We thought we'd grow into it. I always imagined that if I had a girl after my son, this could be her room. My husband or son sometimes use it as an office. I didn't realise it had become so dusty, I haven't been in to clean recently. I haven't had the time.

This is the bedroom my husband and I use. Oh my, I forgot to make the bed this morning. What must you think of me? I'll just pull it straight now, put these tissues in the bin. And if I open the curtains it'll be easier for you to see.

The bathroom. Yes, I agree nowadays showers are much more popular. I haven't used the bath since my son was a toddler but he always loved splashing around in the water. Have you got children? But no, you're much too young. I must admit I was surprised by it when you arrived, but that's how it is for the new generation, all these young girls getting jobs, working. How old are you, if you don't mind me asking? Nevermind, it doesn't matter. And that's it. If you can come another day for photographs I'll be sure to tidy up.

Oh, you're quite right, there's one room left. How did I forget? Here we are. This is where my son and my daughter-in-law were living, but that's all over now. They just didn't get on. I'd suspected for a while, but I'd hoped... She was such a nice girl. My son is staying with a friend at the moment. I told him– We both needed some space.

Yes it is up to date. We got it all done before the wedding, added the en-suite and redecorated. I wanted it to be nice for my daughter-in-law, and you know she did like it. She used to sit here at the dressing table and brush out her hair, put her makeup on, chatting to me the whole time about this and that. I picked the dressing table myself out of a catalogue. It was something I would have loved as a new bride. Something I would have loved for my daughter. You should have seen the room when she was here. Dressing table covered in all her perfume bottles and cosmetics. That wardrobe would barely close with her dresses, all the beautiful bright colours with silver and gold working. A room fit for a princess.

Did you want to look around some more? That's fine, go ahead. Take your time. I think I'll just sit here at the dressing table have a little rest. It's silly but, sometimes I sit here and I forget. I feel like she'll just step out of the bathroom, hair up in a towel, asking me what outfit she thinks she should wear.

I haven't seen her since it all finished. There's so much I didn't tell her. I'm sure she'll come round one of these days to see me. We didn't even have a chance to say goodbye properly. That's the only worry, if the house sells quickly, I'll need to speak to the new owners, so that they can pass on my details when she comes, though I'm sure she'll visit much sooner than that.

Maybe today, even.

Did you hear a knock at the door?

The One Where She Wanted To Break Things

As she trudged up each step, Shazia built another half-argument, imagined another charged up, righteous complaint. By the time she reached the bedroom at the top of the house, the thoughts were coiled up, ready to break loose, attack and wound. She pushed the door open and stood in the doorway. Hasan was sitting on their double bed. He had his back against the headboard with his legs stretched out, watching an old episode of *Friends* on his phone.

'Can you not sit on our bed with dirty clothes?' Shazia said. It was not what she had planned to say, but something else that jumped out without checking with her. 'Who knows what you've picked up on the underground.'

'I was tired.' A canned laugh track spilled out of the phone's speakers. 'I'll change them.'

'It's too late now. I'll wash the bedclothes tomorrow. Not like I have anything better to do.' She looked away from the bed, at the cramped room they lived in. The sloped ceiling met walls that were bare except for a framed wedding invitation. It hung from an exposed nail, above eye level, where the gilt from the gold calligraphy caught the light of the uncovered bulb. She stared at it now. 'We put that frame up too high.'

'What?' Hasan tapped his phone, pausing the video. 'Did you say something?'

'The wedding invitation. It looks stupid up there. You hammered the nail in too high and no one can see it.'

'What?' He started to laugh. Happy, carelessly. 'If no one can see it, how can it look stupid?'

'It does. I see it.'

'You've never said before. Why don't you come and sit.' Hasan patted the bed next to him, pulling up Shazia's pillow against the backrest and smoothing the duvet. 'This one's so funny.'

'What about Saffy? Her nappy needs changing before bed.'

'Mum will do it.'

'I don't want your mum to do it. She does enough.' Shazia found her eyes on the wedding invitation again. 'I can just imagine her telling her friends *'Shazia isn't very capable. I do everything for the child.'*'

'It helps you though.' Hasan tapped play on his phone. 'So why worry?'

'It's not help. She's not doing it for me.' She watched as Hasan's episode finished, and he started another. The upbeat opening music twisted her stomach. 'I'm thinking of visiting my mum. I need a break.'

'We can go this weekend, if you like.'

'Not a weekend. Not you and me.'

Hasan put the phone down and rubbed his eyes, finally looking at her. 'We've talked about this.'

Shazia moved from the doorway, to the rail of clothing jammed against one wall. She seized a black overnight bag hanging from the pole, jangling the railing as she went so the hangers clattered and the clothes swayed, and dumped it on the bed, pushing out the sides so it gaped open.

'Shaz.'

From the rail she selected a few tunic dresses. The tops of the hangers and the shoulders of the dresses looked faded, but it was just dust that transferred to her fingers as she pulled them off, folded them sloppily in mid air and put them in the bag, filling it out. She wiped her fingers on her leggings, leaving grey smears on the fabric and knelt down to a messy collection of baskets tucked under the railing, from which she took socks and underwear.

'Shaz.' He'd moved to sit at the bottom of the bed, next to the bag, pulling something out. 'What are you doing?'

'Don't touch that.' She snatched the dress out of his hands.

'I'm just wondering why you're taking such nice clothes.'

'They're not nice. They're the only things that fit me.' Her old clothes, the smart, bright and fun clothes that couldn't fit her expanded body anymore, had been moved to storage, leaving frumpy, shapeless things that she could hide in. Behind the rail, hastily tucked away, was a growing collection of fast fashion pieces she ordered online, hoping that a new style or print would trigger a magic transformation. *Why do you keep ordering more clothes?'* Hasan's mum had asked her twenty minutes ago while she was wiping down the kitchen table, in a tone that was supposed to be kind, supposed to be encouraging. *'If you lose weight and*

25

fit into the ones you already have, then you'll be able to save money. If you don't work to get your figure back now it'll only get worse with the next one. Look at Hasan's sister: three kids, but she wears size ten.'

Shazia squeezed past the rail of clothes, careful not to brush Hasan's legs as she went, and opened a small chest of drawers. She pulled out a few vests, babygrows and one or two outfits that were already folded into tidy squares, dresses with matching leggings nestled together. Holding them in her arms she shuffled back to the bed, ignoring Hasan watching her, avoiding his eyes as she placed them in the bag.

'Toiletries?' Hasan asked.

'I can pack a bag.'

'I know-'

'You don't!' The clothes in the bag had all jumbled together into a mess that blurred in front of Shazia's eyes. 'You don't have any idea.' She pulled them out to start refolding, keeping her head down. She laid the tunic she had snatched from Hasan, a navy shift with a faded grey pattern, on the bed. It had never looked so plain and miserable, she thought, as she smoothed it down with a shaking hand. She brought each side in, then folded the top into careful thirds, until she held a perfect, neat parcel in her hands. Looking at what she'd created, the tears spilled out.

'Shaz, don't cry.' She couldn't see Hasan but she felt his hands reach for her. She pushed him away, shaking her head. After a few seconds, she heard the creak of the bed as he stood up, and the door open. She turned around, facing

26

the wall and sniffed. The door opened again, and she half turned.

'Here.' Hasan passed her the toiletry bag. She had picked it out five years ago, for their honeymoon, to hold the substantial cosmetics required by a new bride. It was pink with a gold clasp, cold in her hands and even half empty, so much heavier than she had expected. Too heavy.

They sat on the bed in silence, Shazia looking at the toiletry bag that was slowly warming in her hands, Hasan looking at her, holding nothing.

'I can move the frame lower,' Hasan said after a few minutes. 'I shouldn't have put it up so high in the first place.'

'No.' Shazia passed him the toiletry bag. 'I'll do it. Let me go and get the hammer.'

AVI KAUR VIRDEE has been everything from a tailor's apprentice (no, she still can't sew) to an ESOL teacher while continuing on her quest to become a Serious Writer. She currently works as a bookseller for a popular high street book chain, which has a nice synergy to it (and also gets her books at discounted prices – which is better than reams of marking). *Bones of Memory* is her first novel.

Bones of Memory is a story of human endeavour told through the lens of faith in the modern age. A novel about truth, conflict and what it means to be redeemed.

There was once an animal that discovered a space within himself and filled it with an origin that reaches back to before the formation of the stars. Of the unseen hands of an unknowable force who guided this animal to vanquish and then build the world as we know it today – and he built it in layers, one over the other.

Here is Antiquity, buried under Enlightenment, on top of which he built Industrial, on whose bones he erected Digital. And ideas, like ghosts, would travel into each age from the previous one, albeit adapted to suit the time. But what happens when the ghost-idea has exhausted its regenerations yet the world is not done changing? What happens when the old idea reaches its apogee in the newest iteration of the world?

I wrote *Bones of Memory* to find out.

Avi was mentored by Mahsuda Snaith.

Bones of Memory

EMILY LANG Obituary
Spiritual Leader and Healer, whose work provoked as much controversy as adulation.

There are few public figures outside politics that are as widely divisive as Emily Lang, who died this week at the age of 34, was.

Famously reclusive and loathe to engage with the press or speak publically, little is truly known about the founder of the All-Folks' Spiritual Movement.

Lang's followers, however, claim her extraordinary messianic abilities began at the age of six, when, while exploring her surroundings on a family outing, she discovered the mysterious All-Stone; reported by some to be the trigger for her apotheosis and the source of her divine power. For several years Lang was seen without it and the All-Stone's whereabouts remain unknown to this day.

Born in the Peak District town of Matlock in 1984, to her parents Alexander and Eleanor (nee Watson), her childhood was shaped by the sorrow of her younger sister's untimely passing, something she never spoke of but that informed part of the work the All-Folks movement undertook; namely raising money for medical research and volunteering in hospitals.

Lang first came to public attention in 1999, when camcorder footage of her setting foot in Stonehenge, while on a school trip, set the megaliths 'singing' – a phenomenon that was reported to have simultaneously occurred at the nearby Stone Circle and Henge at Avebury and as far away as the great Neolithic monuments on the Isle of Orkney.

Explained away by geologists as an effect of vibratory impact from deep within the earth, it was at this point nevertheless that her following began; her peers, including the future Hollywood A-lister Josie Flowers, becoming the earliest advocates and devotees of the All-Folks movement, learning from her the values of kindness and introspection. 'The Kids Are Alright,' the tabloid commentator Shelley Bastien wrote in early 2001. 'Who on earth has a problem with a generation that grows up to be kind?'

Not everyone was convinced by her authenticity, however; in the high-paranoia of the world post 9/11, Lang and her growing movement were beginning to be treated suspiciously, linked to ever-increasing conspiracy theories circulating online on the one hand, or viewed as the harbinger of the end times on the other.

'They talk of the truth of her words,' the US televangelist Gabriel Schlock once preached to his congregation, 'but beware, for I say to you her words be not the truth but the whisperings of Iblis.'

Beyond the religious communities and conspiracy theorists, Lang really came into prominence in 2005 when a premonition she received while waiting at Bethnal Green train station led to her clearing a train of its passengers, thereby averting a terrorist attack.

Her reputation for piety and her principles for mercy and compassion were attacked at the subsequent criminal inquiry into the attack she foiled, when suggestions began to emerge that she was one of the architects of the would-be atrocity. Though never proven, this event amplified the growing discontent of her detractors; tenuous connections to extremism would dog Lang throughout her public life, something she once famously described as the result of 'an unspoken nexus of race and shame'.

Bolstered by her life-long friendship with Josie Flowers, however, the All-Folks movement saw ever greater numbers sign up.

Ben Highsmith, Administrative Executive of All-Folks UK, referred to this surge in membership as 'proof that the modern age can't provide the balm we need to soothe the soul.'

Indeed, the movement's members took the peace they found through her teachings as evidence of her divinity, some to the extent of such religious fervour that they would force austerities upon themselves as hallmarks of their devotion.

Lang's theological ideologies brought an uneasy adoration, countered by similar levels of scrutiny from across the divide. Unofficial accounts of her spiritual practices began to circulate and although none of the allegations were ever corroborated, or indeed commented on by Lang or her acolytes, the attempts to unmask her as a fraud continued unabated.

'Homegirl could click her fingers and make life on this planet everything we need it to be just like that,' Saira Noor, the radical feminist stand-up comedienne once said, 'you think it doesn't happen cus she'd rather we sat around a fucking campfire singing some Kumbaya bullshit or do you think it doesn't happen because she can't do it?'

Lang countered this argument in a rare foray onto social media, demonstrating both her playful intellect and her love of Star Trek: The Next Generation with the words 'I'm not Q, *Non Capitan*.'
(The 'Non' was not a typo but wordplay that delivered both an answer in the negative and a reminder that Noor is no Captain Picard, just as Lang was not the extra-dimensional antagonist with apparent control over the laws of reality, physics, time and space).

In recent years her name and good works were further tarnished by an FBI investigation into the All-Folks global networks on charges of corruption and people trafficking, triggering an international outcry as millions took to the streets in peaceful protest, shutting down traffic systems across cities worldwide.

The FBI charges were later dropped when no evidence to support them could be found, though the damage was done. Lang announced that she'd dismantled her spiritual networks and went off-grid for several years; although, whether personal testimonies of the lives she helped transform or multi-media opinion pieces decrying her and her movement, the stories about her came rolling in one after the other despite her withdrawal from the world.

Her return to the public sphere this week was tragically cut short when an adoring devotee 'martyred' her before a throng of well-wishers.

'How can it be,' Highsmith wrote yesterday in an attempt to make sense of her passing, 'that one man can be allowed to break so many hearts?'

But perhaps the real measure is the enormous number of hearts that Lang opened, gently, in the first place and encouraged, despite their fear, to bloom.

She is survived by her parents, Alexander and Eleanor.

Emily Charlotte Lang, Spiritual Leader, born 27th October 1984, died 1st April 2019.

Chapter 1: Boyd Miller (The Journalist)

The door to the coffee shop was like a portal to another world.

As soon as he was inside he felt the tip of his nose tingling in shock at the warmth. On the other side of the door the world stood submerged in dense fog, the air so bitter your breath steamed.

It was late July.

He stamped his feet and jostled past the patrons to the counter.

The barista looked at him sullenly; a wildness in her eyes that spoke of approaching ruin.

'Suppose you'll be wanting nettle tea,' she said. 'It's all anyone orders these days. Shan't be much of that to go round neither soon, mark me.'

She stared fearfully out of the windows.

'It's all upside down,' she whispered, mostly to herself. 'It's gone wrong. We shan't survive it for what was done.'

The hair on the back of his neck quivered. There were others like her, many of them, growing more vocal with each passing day. The weather had decimated global harvests and sent the prices of food stocks soaring. People were on edge and the longer the cold remained, the more their fear grew.

He smiled and ordered a coffee, precious commodity now, happily parting with almost fifteen pounds so he could hurry to a table.

'I'll let you know when it's ready. Name?'

'Declan. Thanks.'

A quiet table in a dark corner beckoned to him. He shrugged off his coat and checked his watch. Angela was late, again.

At the table next to his, an old woman with owl-rimmed glasses slammed her newspaper down in disgust.

'Despicable,' she spat toward her male companion. 'Despots and tyrants the lot of them. Have you seen this?'

She jabbed a stubby, nicotine-stained finger at the front page.

'Aye,' he removed his bobble hat and nodded, his fine white hair tufted up with static. 'They're all in league with each other, these politicians and corporations. Always on the make. Public servants, my arse.'

'They want stringing up!' interjected a new voice from somewhere above Declan.

He looked up in alarm. There stood Angela, holding the coffee with his name on it. She placed it on the table. Her hands were gloved in fine leather. He grimaced playfully at her wide grin. Trust her to turn any situation into a vox-pop.

'Don't mind us carping, love,' the old woman nodded at her. 'None of this would happen in us days. There'd be a public outcry. Seems these young don't know what they're about.'

'Too busy staring at screens,' Angela agreed.

'Well they've grown up with all this,' the man said. 'It's normal to 'em. We just didn't share pictures of us children or announce our wealth to the world. If a stranger were to ask what shampoo we used we'd have said 'None of your business."

Angela nodded in sympathy.

Declan looked at his watch pointedly, wondering how much longer Angela would indulge these people.

'Doesn't surprise me at all though, love,' the voice of the barista rang out across the room. 'They're all like that, the people at the top. She told us they were. She was going to show us.'

Angela's face was a mask of innocence.

'Who?'

'Emily Lang.'

The old couple nodded. Murmurs of agreement rumbled around the shop. Declan studied the patrons; such a diverse bunch of people apparently unified by the loss of a public figure. What did the teenage mother over there have in common with the suited young fellow wearing a lanyard round his neck? Or the old, tweed-jacketed man with the air of an eccentric university lecturer? Perhaps it was safety in numbers; nowadays you were better to adopt the majority opinion of wherever you were than face the backlash by swimming upstream.

'I were never convinced by her y'know,' the old lady said. 'But I wished her no ill all a' same. Seemed to me she were giving young folk summat to believe in, encouraging them to be better.'

'Aye,' her companion concurred. 'Look at all that's happened since. It's not right. Seen nuthin like it in all us life. Thick frost in July? Even here the farmers are saying they crops have gone to nowt. There'll be no harvest. We can't keep going on nettle tea forever. Folk will starve.'

'And all the while the turds in power are selling our data for their own profit,' added the barista to general nodding and consent. 'That's just the tip of the iceberg, mark me.'

'Twas ever thus,' Angela shook her head pitifully. 'In her absence thank goodness for people like....'

She picked up the old lady's newspaper and made a show of reading out the journalist's name.

'... Boyd Miller. Without him we'd be none the wiser.'

An uneasy silence fell and Declan drank his coffee. He didn't even like coffee; the day had already irked him.

'Your tea's ready Angela, love,' the barista called. 'Sit down, I'll bring it over.'

'Thanks Natalie.'

Declan looked at her hatefully as she sat and removed her gloves. She glanced over his cup, her eyebrows almost disappearing into her hairline.

'Coffee, eh? How much am I paying you?'

'What was all that about?' he asked, flicking his chin upward.

'Empirical demonstration of public opinion,' she answered sweetly. 'Your report into the despicable activities of Big Tech hasn't landed the way you expected.'

He winced.

'Relax,' she grinned, 'no one can hear me, *Boyd*.'

Her eyebrows rose in playful accompaniment to the emphasis she put on the name.

'I come bearing news.'

'Must you be so indiscreet? What's your news?'

Angela pretended to laugh as Natalie, the barista, brought over her tea tray. He forced himself to beam in response, as though they were old friends catching up.

'There'll be a parliamentary investigation. They'll look to impose fines and put together new policy. We've given the Select committee copies of all you gave us and the legal department sent over the injunction paperwork to protect your identity. You won't have to present yourself before them.'

'They've agreed to that?'

'They had to, we weren't playing ball unless they did.'

He stared at her. She let him look deep into her eyes and smiled serenely.

He cleared his throat.

'Thank you.'

She took a sip of her tea and reached for her bag. He tried not to watch her. Sometimes it seemed to him as though everything she did was designed to be seen. She was less rummaging through her bag than massaging the folds and divides of the fabric; her long, tapered fingers expertly weaving their way through its hidden treasures.

Her hair today seemed to hold an enchanting lustre, holding the light in its deep garnet glow. He wondered whether she'd been to the hairdresser's. He tried not to think of who she reminded him of.

'Got you a present,' she said, placing a thick file on the table before them.

'And by 'present' you of course mean...?'

'Your next assignment.'

He opened the file and looked through the contents. There was no shortage of material; cuttings, photos, lists, pages and pages of information. Handwritten notes in red ink. Highlighted passages in neon. The more he looked at it, the sicker he felt. He closed the file again.

'There's this too,' Angela said, passing him a USB drive. It was so small he almost sent it skittering off the table while trying to pick it up.

'Keep it safe,' she lowered her voice and took another sip of tea.

He shook his head.

'What is this? I don't want it.'

'I need you to look into it for us.'

Suddenly he understood the scene upon her arrival. What was it she said? 'Empirical evidence of public opinion'? Everything she did was designed to be viewed. She was showing him. He'd spent months as a deep insider gathering information; putting together an investigation to expose how corporate technology companies were commodifying the personal data of users and the public response was apathy. They weren't surprised by corruption anymore. They expected it.

'What am I supposed to do?' he hissed. 'The woman is dead!'

Angela eyed him coolly. He let her examine his face deeply and didn't flinch. When she eventually spoke, it was the calm delivery of her words that shook him.

'I want you to find out who killed her.'

He kept his voice steady.

'We know who killed her.'

She picked up the file and put it back in her bag, drained her cup and stood.

'Come with me,' she said.

They drove in silence through the fog, slowly, with plenty of time to see oncoming traffic. It was twilight when they finally reached their destination.

She led him into the aged brick building via the back, a secure pass in her hand remotely deactivating the security lock. A long corridor led to the service lifts. They had a smell he couldn't quite place; an old library or primary school smell, of musty cardboard, of yellowed papers brittle with age.

She ushered him in and pressed level five. It occurred to him that he hadn't noticed any other people, save the two of them.

There was a single door on level five. She swiped her pass and pushed open the door, letting him in. On the inside there were extra security measures; she bolted and chained the door and drew the curtains. It was a large suite, with open fireplaces and opulent furnishing, the interior designer was clearly a fan of fin-de-siècle luxury; the colours were all deep sea greens, vivid blues and mellow greys, punctuated by pops of ochre or dusky rose.

Angela threw off her coat and kept walking.

He followed her to the bedroom.

'Who laid the fire?' he asked, looking at the kindling in the fireplace.

'This is our corporate apartment,' she replied. 'It's secure.'

He noticed she didn't answer the question.

She poured a drink for them both and lit the fire. He was grateful for the warmth and drew nearer to it, grabbing the poker to heighten the flame. The wood snapped and the fire crackled.

When he stood to face Angela she reached her hand up to his neck and stroked his hair. She drew her face down to his and kissed him hungrily.

'I've missed you,' she whispered into his mouth as he unzipped her dress.

He didn't reply.

Afterward they lay in bed together, and he marvelled at the way the thin sheen of her sweat made her skin glow. He kissed the space between her breasts and she smiled down to him, lazily. Her fingers played with his hair and she cradled him to her, as though she needed to keep him safe.

He carefully disentangled himself from her limbs and rolled off her body, conscious she may not be able to bear the weight of him much longer.

'Well, you seem okay,' she said after a pause and he chuckled.

'Thanks for the aftercare,' he quipped.

'You're welcome,' she replied after the briefest hesitation.

The mood changed; suddenly they were awkward with each other. She threw off the covers and strode into the en-suite, locking the door behind her.

Declan picked up his clothes and made his way to the master bathroom.

When he returned, he found Angela sat on the bed with a robe wrapped around her. She'd removed the file from her bag again and thrown it onto the covers next to the notebook laptop she was using.

'Come and sit down,' she said to him without looking, 'I'll just be a minute. You still have that USB drive?'

He patted down his clothes then remembered it was in the inside zip-pocket of his coat.

She plugged it in and brought up some files.

'Read this,' she said, handing him the notebook.

He sighed and shook his head. Her persistence was irritating. There was something cheap and somehow tawdry about what she was asking him to do; he couldn't reconcile it with his journalistic integrity – or what he knew about hers.

'Oh, stop it with the pious stance,' Angela rolled her eyes. 'There's a story here, we're not cashing in on someone's devastation. The file holds detailed information about Emily Lang's life and activities. The electronic files on this device include a list of people who had an unhealthy interest in her. You may recognise some of the names.'

Declan gawked at the screen and scanned the list of names. He inhaled sharply and looked at Angela, who beamed at him.

He shook his head again, a soft smile playing on his lips.

'This can't be conjecture.'

'It's not. Follow the trail and you'll find the solid lead. What's your gut telling you?'

There it was: Angela's intuitive knowing for where the truth lay. Professionally, she could read him like a book. Personally, he was still a work-in-progress for her, just as he wanted.

'Let's nail the bastard.'

She nodded, then put a hand on his arm. A furrow appeared between her eyebrows, her lips suddenly pressed thin.

'The whole picture though, Declan. This isn't going to be 'Boyd's Vendetta'. You uncover the entire mystery, one veil at a time.'

He nodded, his mind racing already through a thousand synaptic connections of names and faces and reputations.

Angela brought him back to reality by opening another file on the screen and handing him the notebook. It was a few pages of a word-processed document.

He raised an eyebrow quizzically. Angela laughed in response.

'A gift from my friend at Gilman-Moorhouse,' she said. 'It's part of an early draft of Josie Flower's memoir.'

He jerked incredulously at that, unsure of where to even begin.

'The best friend? Isn't she a bit young to be releasing a memoir?'

'Apparently not young enough for Hollywood anymore,' Angela replied, savouring the gossip. 'I hear the job offers aren't as frequent as they used to be so she's decided to cash in while the interest is still hot.'

He found the glee with which she relayed this information somehow distasteful and mildly needling. He picked up the notebook and sat on the floor to read the document, moving away from her.

Angela disrobed and began to dress, running her hands over the material of her clothes before slipping them on. Declan recalled an old TV image of a naked woman robed in a milky white sheet of shining silk. He struggled to recall where it came from. An advert for chocolate?

Angela's little show was doing nothing for him; he fixed his eyes to the notebook screen and began to read.

There's a peculiar hatred of adulthood that manifests itself through the way we reflect on our childhoods. We imagine things were better when we were young; the skies were bluer, the sweets tasted better, the world itself was altogether kinder and more innocent and we were happier for this simpler, somehow more authentic time.

For the most part, this is a lie.

My childhood was marred early on by the messy breakdown of my parent's marriage.

I remember that time as bleak and grey. I am an only child and had nobody with whom I could share the horror of my parents' mutual contempt for each other. Each evening was like a demented performance of Who's Afraid of Virginia Woolf *meets* Whatever Happened to Baby Jane, *with each of them playing each role interchangeably. Little wonder I became an actor when every night I witnessed the spectacle of each of them competing to be the most vile, remembering me only when one of them needed a pawn to torment the other with.*

Concerned neighbours called the police. Social services removed me from the house. My father's parents were long gone; retired abroad to enjoy their remaining years in the Mediterranean sunshine. My mum's parents were still young and strong. When the court awarded them parental responsibility, they spirited me away to a different city, a happier home, a new start.

And a new school, where I met Emily.

It was 1990. Being from a broken home wasn't nearly as common-place as it is now. You must know how cruel children can be when you

45

stick out; with Nan and Gramps doing the school run every day, word soon got around.

My earliest memories of Emily are captured in two moments that I still remember vividly. I can still see that concrete playground: boys kicking a ball around, children shrieking, playing Tig or racing each other up and down the yard.

I am boxed in by a gang of girls whose names I barely remember now. Emily is one of them. They are asking me about my parents, my grandparents. I don't know why I'm telling them. I want them to like me, I suppose.

They're not being explicitly cruel to me but there is a hunger in their wanting to know, a kick they get from my not realising I'm arming them with the weapons they will use to hurt me. They're like crocodiles just covered by the surface of the water, waiting for that young buck turned foolish from thirst.

They do not plague me but now and then I catch the flicker of a smile passing from one face to another. This smile isn't friendly and it frightens me.

And then I look at Emily. She isn't asking me questions. She isn't really interested in the answers. She looks fed up. I remember the contagious smile turning to surprise when she says, quietly but firmly enough to be heard, 'Leave her alone.'

We are six years old.

'Are you fast?' she asks me. 'I'll race you to the dinner hall.'

I remember her laugh as I set off at speed, catching her off-guard. My fringe is in my eyes when I reach the dinner hall. I turn to smile at her gratefully. She's only a foot behind me and her grin is the first bright thing I remember.

The second memory is from a few months later. Emily and I are friends now and regularly see her little sister Molly in the nursery playground when we're all on morning break together. She always waves at me and shouts my name across the yard, 'Johhhhhssieeeeee!' She knows I'll pull a funny face at her to make her laugh.

The day of this memory, though, she doesn't wave at me. I run right to the boundary line separating the nursery playground from the juniors' and make a funny face for her but she doesn't laugh.

'Are you still feeling poorly?' Emily asks, stood by my shoulder. Her dark eyebrows are knitted together in concern. Molly nods her head. Her lips quiver. Emily kneels to hug her sister and I am envious of the love they get to share by virtue of being siblings. Molly hugs Emily tight and cries. Emily wipes her sister's tears and Molly's nose runs with blood.

I feel my gut contract and my spine flex, like when a snowball shatters on your neck and slips down your collar, under your clothes.

Emily is frantically putting a tissue to Molly's nose. I have clamped my hands firmly over my mouth.

Molly is so little and so young.

More children are gathering now, drawn by Molly's screams.

'Get a teacher!' Emily yells at them. She stands to search her pockets for another tissue and the moment she lets go of her sister I can see Molly's going to fall. I can sense it; my skin twitches and tingles with the knowing.

47

In a flash I'm there to catch her. A teacher bumbles through the crowd as Emily cries, trying to rouse her sister. There is blood on my coat sleeve. More teachers gather round.

Emily is panicked now and weeping. I put my free arm around her. The sky is grey.

'Do we know what happened to the little sister?' Declan asked in the car. Angela had agreed to drop him somewhere public from where he'd make his own way home.

'Leukaemia,' Angela shook her head. 'She didn't make it.'

'Jesus.'

He was quiet, reflecting once more on what a cold, hard bastard the world truly was.

'Why did she write about it?' he thought out loud. 'If people already know this about the sister, why did Josie Flowers put it in *her* memoir about *her* friendship with Emily?'

'Why not open with that question tomorrow?' Angela shrugged, taking her eyes off the road for a moment to face him.

'She's agreed to an interview. I've written the details in the file under her info.'

He shook his head, exasperated. How typical of Angela to spring crucial details on him like it was no big deal.

'I could have used a little time to prepare,' he chided her.

'Quite a nerd, aren't you?' she goaded, good-naturedly. 'Well then you shouldn't have allowed me to get so distracted.'

She grinned, turning to flash him a wink.

He snorted and stared out of the window, kissed to an icy crisp by the frost.

NAZIRA VANIA is a Leicester-based writer and social worker. Her love of writing began in her younger years, but after completing The Asian Writer's Becoming a Writer course she decided that it was time to start sharing her words with the world. Nazira's story 'Numbers' was subsequently shortlisted for the Leicester Writes Short Story Prize in 2018.

Like the central character in her novel *When You're Smiling*, Nazira supports Leicester City Football Club and can often be found at their stadium with her son, cheering them on and losing her voice in the process. Her somewhat less vociferous pastimes include cooking, reading, knitting, and buying stationery that she really doesn't need. She can be found on Twitter @nazvanz.

'Kick Off' is the opening chapter of my novel *When You're Smiling*, a vibrant, witty, and politically astute football-themed tale that crosses *Mrs Dalloway* with *Fever Pitch* and *Bend It Like Beckham*. The novel is set in 2016 on the day that Leicester City Football Club won the Premier League title, and it brings together a vibrant cast of characters to explore themes of family, identity, belonging, and triumph over adversity. 2016 was also the year of the referendum on the UK leaving Europe.

Watching Leicester's fairy-tale season unfolding alongside the build up to the big vote, I was fascinated by the contrast in the rhetoric surrounding the two events.

Whereas the Leicester story was about unity, diversity, and working together to overcome challenges, the Brexit story was about separation, closing borders, and going it alone. Observing this, I was inspired to write a novel that captured the mood and contradictions in the city and country at the time. I had also long been playing with the concept of a modern, urban, diverse update on *Mrs Dalloway*, so I brought the two ideas together and *When You're Smiling* was born.

Nazira was mentored by Kerry Young.

Kick Off

'Good morning Filbert.'

Hasina Fayrouz steps into the paved back yard of her red-brick terrace home and places a bowl on the ground. A cat darts out from behind a potted rose bush and lunges for the milk. Hasina watches him with a twinge of guilt.

'Sorry I'm late, love. I got carried away reading things on my phone.' She bends forward and lowers her voice. 'You know how it is Filbert. Too much Twitter on the shitter.'

The cat pauses mid-lap and stares at her.

Hasina feels deservingly reprimanded. 'Sorry duck.'

Filbert dives back into his breakfast. Hasina straightens up and pulls her gown tight against the early-morning chill. She must stop talking with him like this, but she sometimes finds herself with things she wants to say and no one to whom she can say them. Especially in recent weeks.

'Time for your daily briefing, Filbo. We got just the one point yesterday but I'm not worried. In fact, I think there's a really good chance Spurs will bottle it tonight and the title will be ours.'

She waits for Filbert to lap up the last of the milk, then continues. 'What do you think boyo? Is Leicester going to do it? Give me one meow for *yes* or two for *no*.'

Filbert flops onto his back for an intimate grooming session. Hasina averts her gaze. If that is meant to be his opinion, she has no idea how to interpret it. She was hoping he secretly possessed some prophetic powers, like the oracular octopus that had correctly predicted winners in the 2010 World Cup. She will just have to discover Leicester's fate the old-fashioned way.

'Right then Filbo, I will give you some privacy. See you later lad.'

Hasina stoops to retrieve the emptied bowl from the ground, then goes into the kitchen.

'You need to stop feeding that cat.'

Hasina jumps. 'Assalaamu'alaykum Mum. You're down early.'

Nasima is standing at the window, staring outside. 'Have you seen how fat it has gotten lately?'

Hasina fills the kettle and tries to quell a newly arrived pang of guilt. She hasn't been blind to Filbert's increasing girth and is well aware that she is at fault. She knew from the day he turned up at their back door that he wasn't a stray, but she grew fond of his company and unofficially adopted him anyway. When Nasima learned of this, after noticing how they kept running out of milk, she wasn't impressed: *'You could always move to your own place if you want a pet that desperately.'* Hasina's chest had tightened at those words. She wasn't, and still isn't, quite ready for that yet.

'Why do they have to lick themselves like that?'

Hasina takes the question as rhetorical. 'Do you want toast or cereal, mum?'

'In my garden as well. It's disgusting.' Nasima tears herself away from the window and seats herself at the table with a newspaper. 'Toast today.'

Hasina pops two slices of bread into the toaster, then switches on the radio.

'It is eight o'clock on the second of May twenty-sixteen! The May Day bank holiday, and what could be a historical one for the city! It was a draw for the Foxes at Manchester United yesterday, but they could still clinch the title in just under fourteen hours' time!'

Nasima looks up from her newspaper. 'Do we have listen to this?'

'Yes mum, we do.'

'City's only challengers, Tottenham Hotspurs, have to beat Chelsea tonight to stay in the race! If they lose or draw, Leicester are crowned Premier League champions! What do you think will happen? Call in with your predictions after the news!'

'They're so worked up, they're practically breathless.' Nasima tuts and shakes her head. 'They'll give themselves heart attacks at this rate.'

Hasina stays tight-lipped. They have been through this a million times. She is tired of having to defend both the game and her right to hear about it.

'Come on, Hasina. Switch it off, please. It's giving me a headache.'

Hasina reaches over to the radio and turns it up. Nasima scowls and shifts her attention to tackling a Sudoku in the newspaper. Hasina smiles. It is not often that she emerges the victor from their battles. She puts on a second round of toast and butters up the first.

On the radio, the news bulletin ends. John from Barrow-Upon-Soar calls in to express his hopes Chelsea to win.

'I can't take this any longer! I just want it to be over.'

'We know how you feel, John! Our bottoms are sore from sitting on the edge of our seats!'

Barry from Broughton Astley chimes in next with his wish.

'Spurs for the win tonight mate. I'd rather see us win the title when we play Everton on Saturday. Seal the deal in front of the home crowd.'

'You've got a good point there, Barry! After the season City have had it would be nice to see them win it for themselves! Not get it by default because Spurs don't win their game this evening!'

'It would certainly set up a nail-biting finish to the title race.'

'I'm not sure I have the nails left for that, Barry! I chewed them all down ages ago!'

One caller after another lines up for airtime. Dave from Hinckley. Mary from Knighton. Steve from Burton-On-The-Wolds. Mark from Glenfield. And Glen from Markfield. Some of them share their predictions, hopes, and wildest dreams, while others meander joyfully along football-paved memory lanes.

Hasina prepares a pot of tea and embarks on a little trip of her own.

'Hello Yunus Mama!'

Nasima claps Hasina on the back. 'We say assalaamu'alaykum, Hasina, not hello. You are seven years old. You should know that by now.'

Hasina shrugs. Hello, salaam. Salaam, hello. What's the difference?

Hellomu'alaykum.

Hasina holds back a giggle. She had better not say it out loud. That would be asking for trouble. She apologises to her mum, then starts again.

'Assalaamu'alaykum Yunus Mama.'

'Walaykumussalaam Hasina.'

Hasina turns to his wife. 'Assalaamu'alaykum Sumayyah Mami.'

'Please Hasina, call me aunty.'

Hasina looks at Sumayyah with knitted brows. How can 'hello' be wrong but 'aunty' be allowed? These grownups and their rules are very confusing.

Next to her, Nasima frowns. But she doesn't say anything. Sumayyah doesn't like anything to be said. Yunus leaves the room and returns with a parcel. He hands it to her, causing the frown to give way to lit-up eyes. The package is the reason for her midweek visit to Yunus. He has just returned from a business trip to India, which means letters and gifts from her family have arrived with him. It is her Christmas, with Yunus cast in the role of Santa.

Nasima opens the parcel. She takes the bundle of letters from the top of the package and puts it straight into her handbag, then explores the other contents. As usual, her parents have sent a dress for their granddaughter.

'How delightful,' Sumayyah exclaims. 'Are you going to model it for us, Hasina?'

Nasima promptly unwraps the dress from its bag. A question from Sumayyah is synonymous with an order.

Hasina backs away. Nasima raises her hand. Hasina remembers its earlier action and thrusts her arms into the air. Nasima yanks off Hasina's old dress and slides on the new one. Hasina looks down at herself. The dress is splattered with green and pink swirls, like somebody has mashed together mint and strawberry ice-cream, and it has lots of shiny yellowy-gold things stuck all over it. She has never seen anything so ugly in her life.

'Oh, it's beautiful, Hasina!' Nasima appraises her with sparkling eyes. 'It is a bit big but you can grow into it for Eid.'

'Your Hasina never has a problem growing into things.' Sumayyah turns to Hasina and smiles. 'Do you?'

Hasina hesitates. She does not know why, but Aunty Sumayyah's words have made her feel kind of yucky inside. She looks to Nasima for a clue on how to respond. That just confuses her more. Nasima is staring ahead with a too-wide smile. It looks like it has been drawn onto her face.

Hasina raises her arms. 'Can you take it off now please mummy?' The dress is itching like crazy and she can't bear to spend another minute inside it. She hates clothes from India. Nasima removes it gently, folds it carefully, then places it into a large tote bag with the other items from the parcel. Hasina grabs her old dress from the floor and gets it on before they make her model something else.

Sumayyah returns her attention to Nasima. 'Did Javed not fancy joining us today?'

Nasima answers quickly. 'He is working.'

'Such a shame,' Sumayyah sighs. 'Who knew that driving buses could be such a time-consuming occupation?'

Yunus touches Sumayyah lightly on the arm, then says something to Nasima in Gujarati. The rest of the conversation continues the same way. Hasina watches without really listening. They speak too quickly, making it hard for her to understand what they are saying. Not that she cares, because it isn't them that she comes to see.

She waits until it looks like they have forgotten her, then slowly backs into the hallway and tiptoes up the stairs to locate her best friend. She finds him sitting on the floor of his bedroom with what looks like photos laid out in front of him.

'Hellomu'alaykum Osman.'

'Hi Hasina.'

Osman doesn't look up from what he is doing. He doesn't even notice her new way of greeting him. He just keeps playing with the photos. Whatever he is doing with them, it doesn't look like much fun. There must be something better to do.

Hasina wanders over to Osman's bookcase. He has a lot of books in his room, and they are all his own, to keep forever. Hasina only has a few books at home. She has to borrow most of what she reads from the library. Which she doesn't mind so much, because it is her favourite place in the world. But she would still love to have a collection like Osman's at home, so that she would never run out of things to read.

She selects a book and takes it over to him. 'Come on Osman, let's play.'

He doesn't look up. 'Play what?'

'Library Library.'

'Not right now.'

'Why?'

'Because I'm busy.'

Hasina squats beside him. 'What are you busy with?'

'Stickers.'

'What kind of stickers?'

'Football ones.'

She watches him shuffle them around some more and tries to work out the point of his activity. There doesn't appear to be one. 'Forget about that, Osman. Let's play Teacher Teacher.'

'I don't want to play Teacher Teacher.'

'How about House House then?'

'No!'

'Why not?' Hasina looks at Osman through narrowed eyes. What is wrong with him? He always enjoys playing those games with her.

'Cos it's boring.'

She feels a bubbling inside. 'House House is not boring!'

'Yes it is!' Osman stands and looks down at her. 'Your games are boring and stupid!'

Hasina straightens up and uses her two extra years' worth of height to look down on him in return. 'My games are not stupid. You're stupid!'

'No, you are!' Osman turns red. 'And I don't want to play your stupid, boring, girly games!'

Hasina flinches. Each word Osman speaks feels like a slap to the face. Her hand flies through the air and returns his attack. It is still holding the book. The corner of the hardback slams into his jaw. Skin splits. Blood spurts out.

Osman looks at her, stunned.

Three seconds of impeccable silence pass between them.

Then he draws a deep breath, closes his eyes, and screams.

The grownups come pounding up the stairs and get stuck in the doorway trying to rush in at once.

Sumayyah is the first to break through. She pushes Hasina aside and scoops Osman into her arms. 'STAY AWAY FROM MY SON!'

Yunus grabs a towel to mop up the blood. Nasima grabs Hasina and delivers a burst of sharp slaps to her bottom, alongside a cascade of apologies to Osman and his parents.

Tears sting Hasina's eyes. She is taken by the arm and dragged out of the bedroom before she gets the chance to cry them. Osman's brother and sister watching the scene from the landing and having a good laugh. Nasima escorts

Hasina past them and down the stairs, pausing only to collect the bags before leading her out of the house.

As they round the corner onto East Park Road, Nasima comes to an abrupt halt. She stoops to meet Hasina's eyes. 'You are a bad girl, Hasina Fayrouz! Just you wait until I tell your father.' Then she turns and begins an angry and silent march home.

Hasina half runs, trying to keep up. 'I'm sorry mummy.'

Nasima doesn't respond. Hasina doesn't repeat the apology. She knows better. She is in serious trouble. Especially when her dad finds out. She seethes. This is all Osman's fault. How dare he call her boring and stupid? *He* is the boring one. *He* is the stupid one. And who is he to call her girly? He couldn't take *one* little hit. He couldn't take one *tiny* spot of blood. He even screamed for his mummy. He is the girly one!

In what feels like seconds they reach Spinney Hill Park. Hasina's heart sinks. She wishes they had never left it to go to Yunus Mama's in the first place. Nasima keeps them moving. They pass the play area and reach the hill. Hasina looks to the top. Home is just beyond the gate. So is her father.

Her tummy starts to feels funny.

He is not going to be happy.

Her legs grow heavy.

He is going to be furious.

Her heart beats faster.

More-angry-than-mummy angry.

Her chest feels tight.

He is going to punish her. With a very big punishment.

She comes to a standstill. 'The hill is too high, mummy. I need a rest.'

Nasima, still silent, walks back down the hill. She grips Hasina's wrist, turns, and recommences her ascent. Hasina is jerked forward. It feels like her arm might be torn from her body. She tries to stay up close to her mum and reduce the pull. It is too hard.

'Slow down, mummy!' Tears make their way down her cheeks. 'Please mummy, it hurts!'

Nasima continues apace. Hasina's plea has dissolved on contact with the air. She looks around for help, but the children are in madrassah and the mums are at home cooking their evening meals.

They reach the crest of the hill and exit the park, then cross Mere Road and turn onto their street. They are at their doorstep in an instant. Nasima unlocks it and lets them in. Hasina's heart goes cold. She was hoping he had been delayed at work, so that her mum would have time to calm down and decide that he doesn't need to be told after all. Like on those other occasions when she tells Hasina, *Let's keep this between me and you.*' But it is too late for that. His work boots are already home. Which means he is there too.

One of the boots is on its side by the wall. The other is lying upside down half way across the front room floor. He always kicks them off and walks away when he gets in. And Nasima always straightens them up when she passes them, which she does now. Hasina shuts the door as Nasima dumps the parcel on the settee, then takes the bundle of envelopes out of her handbag and tucks them into the gas meter cupboard before going into the living room.

Hasina doesn't follow. She feels safer by the exit. And she doesn't have to be in the same room as them to know what is being said. She hears him being filled in on the afternoon's events. She hears words that don't sound nice. *Stupid girl. Haraami. Shameful.* And then, she hears him.

'HASINA!'

She tries to respond. Her mouth refuses to make a sound.

'HASINA, GET IN HERE RIGHT NOW!'

Her feet fail to move. She is frozen to the floor.

'HASINA!'

She can't do it. She just can't.

Less than a heartbeat later, she doesn't have to. Not prepared to have his summons ignored, Javed comes charging out of the living room. His face is twisted. His left hand is raised.

Hasina knows what is coming, but it hits her full across the face before she can stop it.

'How dare you!'

His right hand comes next and gives her a matching burn in her other cheek.

'How dare you behave like that?!'

Hasina's eyes prickle. She tries not to succumb to what is behind them. He only gets angrier when she cries.

His hand comes at her again. A lot heavier this time, onto her arm. The force knocks her sideways and breaks her frozen feet off the floor, like an icicle off the edge of a roof. She hits the wall and slides down onto the carpet, landing beside his neatly-lined-up boots.

'Is there any reason you're staring at me, Hasina?'

'Oh.' Hasina returns to her surroundings. 'No. Sorry mum. I was just… lost in thought.'

'Well get unlost, dear. The breakfast won't serve itself.'

Hasina takes the tea and toast to the table, then sits down opposite Nasima. She stirs her tea and attempts a sip. It is too hot. She goes for a nibble of toast instead.

The chatter on the radio continues in the same vein. The caller is talking about his first Leicester match, at the age of five. It was an intergenerational affair: grandad, dad, son. Women, it seemed to Hasina, rarely featured in these scenarios, except when credited as the knitters of the team-colours scarves.

The caller describes the nerves that engulfed him in the week before the big day, and the excitement that gripped him the night before.

'It left me so tired that I nodded off during a lull in the game. Next thing I know, I was woken by this massive roar. We'd only gone and scored!'

His happiness was short-lived, he says, as Leicester's goal was followed up with two from the opposing side.

'I cried all the way home. Grandad said I had better get used to it if I was going to be a Leicester fan. And I very quickly did.' The caller laughs so hard, it turns into a wheezing cough. *'It weren't half miserable sometimes, following the Blue Army. And I don't mind telling you mate, I've cried many, many times since that first game. But it has never once entered my mind to support another team.'*

Hasina starts on a second piece of toast. The caller's football-fandom origin story is so very different to hers, just like the many other anecdotes shared over the airwaves. Those have all been yarns spun of more wholesome stuff, like flat caps and bobble hats and half-time pies. She is yet to hear an account featuring books, blood, and a beating. She doesn't imagine for one moment that she is the only person to have been introduced to the beautiful game in such a hideously ugly way, but has no way to tell how common it is, either. After all, people with such experiences are not exactly going to feel inclined to call up the station with their tales.

'Lost in thought again, Hasina? What's wrong?'

Hasina grips her mug and lowers her head. 'Nothing.'

'What's the matter?'

Hasina dabs at the corners of her eyes with the edge of her sleeve. It was silly to think the tears wouldn't be spotted. She takes a sip of tea, along with a moment to compose her response. 'It's just this football stuff, mum. It brings up memories.'

Nasima points at the radio. 'Give that thing a rest then, seeing as it makes you so miserable.'

'It's not the radio's fault, mum. And I'm not miserable. I'm happy. Honest. This season has been amazing! It's just... Well... It also makes me think of... You know.'

Nasima looks at Hasina steadily, as if contemplating her words. Then she drains the last of her tea and stands. 'I have to get ready for my lesson.'

Hasina glances at the clock. 'It's only half-past-eight, mum. That starts at ten.'

Nasima places her mug on the table, turns, and leaves the kitchen.

Hasina watches her walk away.

She should have stuck with talking to the cat.

DR SHAHED YOUSAF is a GP who works in prisons and is the author of two medical books. His writing has diversified over the past few years to include flash fiction, short stories and a novel. He was shortlisted for the Bath Flash Fiction Prize 2016 and commended for the Faber & Faber FAB prize 2017. He undertook the Penguin Random House Constructing a Novel creative writing course as well as short story and flash fiction master classes.

Shahed won a place on to both the Middle Way Mentoring Project 2019 and the Writing West Midlands Room 204 programme 2019. He is a passionate believer in people working together to achieve incredible goals. Mentoring has already been invaluable to his writing and he was a panellist at the National Writers' Conference on The Value of Mentoring in June 2019. In March 2020 his flash fiction 'Zero Tolerance' appeared in Raven Chronicles Press's Anthology, Take a Stand: Art Against Hate.

Welcome to Hell gives an insider's account of the extraordinary world of prisons and the justice system. Each chapter centres on a different prisoner and the challenges they face. The prison service and the NHS have never been under such strain from understaffing and lack of funds. These are difficult times but what keeps staff from coming back day after day? Ultimately this is a story of hope. Although it is dark it is illuminated by many acts of kindness and humour.

As the story unfolds the doctor realises he has more to fear from his employers than the prisoners. He becomes concerned that the prison has the highest death rate of any prison in the UK and decides to 'whistle blow'. He is wrongly accused of fraud and suspended from work. If criminal charges are proven he could be sentenced to a prison term. He has no option but to overcome his fear and fight to clear his name. He takes his employers to an employment tribunal and pursues a case of bullying and harassment against them. He must represent himself in the fourteen day trial. During the trial it emerges that his employers have broken numerous laws in order to silence him as a 'whistle-blower'.

The shocking conclusion is that despite the evidence of the doctor's innocence and the unlawful activity of his employers the judge finds in their favour. The doctor loses his faith in the concept of legal justice and it makes him question if he can continue in his passion of working in prisons? The end of the novel is unfortunately true of the experiences of many medical practitioners who 'whistle-blow' to protect their patients and are themselves harassed and face ruin.

Shahed was mentored by Susmita Bhattacharya.

Mr Freddie Mercury

Mr Freddie Mercury had changed his name by deed poll. He was previously Michael Jackson and before that Sir Elton John. Most prisoners were identified by prison numbers which were printed on their ID cards and must be carried at all times. Mr Mercury was not a number; he broke rules, fought, took drugs. He had served fifteen years for a three year prison sentence and did not meet any of the criteria to show he was reformed and rehabilitated. It was an interminable cycle of bad behaviour and punishment. He was deemed a danger to himself and the public.

Imprisonment for Public Protection (IPP) sentences, like Mr Mercury's, had been abolished by the European Court of Human Rights in 2012 as a human rights violation. The abolishment was not retrospective and Mr Mercury and thousands of others like him languished in hopelessness. As a prison doctor all I could do was stitch his wounds. I was called to the Inpatient Unit, otherwise referred to as the Hospital wing, to see him. Mr Mercury was on a constant watch observation. An officer was monitoring him through the glass observation panel in the cell door. It was his job to make regular entries in the Assessment, Care in Custody, Teamwork (ACCT) document. The officer was known as Ginge, he was ex-services, always incredulously cheerful.

'What's up, Doc?' he asked as I approached.

'Another day in Paradise mate! What is it this time the hands or the feet?' I asked.

'The spoon,' Ginge said.

I exhaled noisily and tried to imagine the damage Mr Mercury could do to himself with a spoon.

'Why does he do it Doc?' Ginge asked.

'Can I see your hands?' I said.

Ginge held out his hands with some hesitation and I examined his nails.

'You and Mr Mercury both bite your nails. The difference is that he is an autocannibal and he swallows his fingernails. He eats his hair, his fingers, his toes and ears,' I said.

Ginge withdrew his hands with a look of disgust.

'Why haven't you taken the spoon off him?' I asked Ginge.

'It was the Governor's decision.'

I felt a tap on my shoulder and I turned to see Nurse Vicky standing beside me. Vicky was the Inpatient Unit manager and was quick to remind me that she was a mental health nurse and did not like blood. The glass in the observation panel had been smashed and our shoes crunched as we stepped closer to the door. We watched Mr Mercury who, despite his long history of eating himself, was morbidly obese with great folds of fat bulging around his body. He was sitting on his bed, naked apart from his stained underwear. Both of his ears had been sliced off and he had missing fingers and toes. There was a deep gash on his left inner thigh and he was scraping the fat from his bloodied muscle with a plastic spoon and eating it. The blood trickled down his leg and congealed on the floor. He did not appear to be in any discomfort. Quite the opposite; he appeared to be in a trance.

'Doesn't that make you feel sick?' Vicky whispered with her hand over her mouth.

'Luckily I am not squeamish,' I responded.

'Mr Mercury is a hostage-taker, you can't go in alone,' Ginge said.

I whispered thank you when an additional officer arrived and the door was unlocked.

'Good luck,' Ginge said.

The door swung open and a wave of hot stench washed over me and I staggered back. It smelt like a butcher's shop; lard and blood. There was also the unmistakeable odour of faeces. It was a sweltering summer day and yet the heating was on at maximum capacity. The prison's thermostat was controlled miles away by someone who was either a sadist or shockingly negligent. The cells were roasting in summer and freezing in winter so the prisoners were either at risk of heatstroke or pneumonia. There were so many layers of madness in a prison it was surprising more prisoners did not lose their minds completely. With a population of over a thousand there were only seventy prisoners on ACCT documents.

'Hi Mr Mercury, I am Dr Y. Can I come in?' I asked as I stood in the doorway and breathed through my mouth.

'I said no Pakis and no Muslims!' Mr Mercury yelled.

I was winded for a moment by the racist gut punch. Any difference in a prison could be exploited and weaponised; all races became slurs, women were called bitches or lezzas and men were accused of being gay. You had to have a thick skin to work in this environment. One of the reasons I chose prison medicine was because I wanted to toughen myself up. Prison taught me to fight.

I wondered why Mr Mercury assumed I was a Muslim other than my brown skin tone? I did not have a beard or any other signifiers of my Islamic faith. I laughed it off but the P word stung. I had been called a black bastard before but I managed to sidestep the intended offence because I was unsure if I was considered black? Did Black in the political sense encompass all non-white people? Was the world divided neatly into the binaries of black and white? In my hierarchy of slurs the N word trumped all insults and had he called me that I would have walked away in disgust and let him bleed.

Vicky raised her voice to admonish him; 'Mr Mercury, the NHS will not tolerate intolerance. Is that clear!'

'Shut up you fake plastic bitch' he yelled.

'Don't forget this 'fake plastic bitch' gives you your medications! I am sick and tired of you insulting staff. This ends now. Do you understand?' She retorted.

He scoffed and there was blood trickling from his mouth. How could I be offended by someone like him?

'I am the only doctor working today. You can either see me or wait until tomorrow?' I said in a conciliatory tone.

'I am not stopping you,' Mr Mercury said and licked his spoon.

'Great,' I said half-heartedly and followed the officers into the cell avoiding the large blood clots on the floor.

Prison was almost entirely grey. Grey cement floors, grey painted brick, grey tracksuits and grey faces. All of the cells were approximately eight feet by ten feet. Mr Mercury filled the room making it appear far smaller. His single bed was secured to the floor in the corner. There was no way someone of his size could fit in a single bed. There was no provision for double beds in prison. The majority of prisoners shared cells and slept in tiny bunk-beds. If a prisoner was grossly obese, like Mr Mercury, they would be advised to put their mattress on the floor and sleep there, if there was space.

The room was stagnant with the reek of his unwashed body and infected ulcers. I wandered how I was going to get close enough to do his stitches? I tried to push the small window open to let some fresh air in but it was nailed shut. The air vents on either side of the window had been painted over and they were blocked and redundant. The sun was shining outside and yet he kept his room dark by covering the windows with newspaper. He was illuminated from the overhead light which made his skin seem almost translucent and he reminded me of a painting by Francis Bacon.

Prisoners were encouraged to personalise their cells to make them homely on their limited budget of seven pounds a week. A bright collage of images was plastered to the wall beside his bed. Blu tack and chewing gum were contraband in prison and the pictures had been secured in place with toothpaste. It leaked through the images like fresh bruises. The happy families and beautiful beach holidays had shadows eating into their hearts. I looked closer and realised what I had assumed were personal photographs had been cut from magazines. He had superimposed photographs of his huge head on to the men's bodies in a heart breaking collage of wishful thinking.

I had to turn away because his misery was leaking into me like toothpaste on a photograph. I cleared my throat and tried to find something positive in this hellhole. He had a pile of books beside his bed; mostly novels by Stephen King and Dean Koontz.

'You like horror?' I asked.

'Can't you tell?' He replied and smiled to reveal dark gums and missing teeth. No horror story could compete with his existence.

'I used to like horror and fantasy too,' I said quietly.

'Not anymore?' He asked.

I shook my head.

'Because of this place?' He asked.

'Yep,' I replied.

Mr Mercury had made excellent soap sculptures of teddy bears and skulls which surrounded him like a substitute family. He was very talented at carving. Beside the toilet stood a life sized model of a brown puppy with its red tongue sticking out. The eyes were rendered in beautiful detail and I reached down to pat its head.

'Don't touch it!' He snapped.

I stepped back.

'I don't have paints,' he said softening his tone.

It was only then that I noticed the brown dog smelt of poo and the tongue was the colour of dry blood. I recoiled in disgust.

'It's a Poodle,' he said and laughed.

'That's sick,' Ginge said.

'What do you expect? The officers don't let me have crayons and colouring pencils because I keep eating them and putting them inside my wounds. But the thing is nothing feels as good as hurting myself. I feel better as soon as I see the blood leave my body,' he said.

I had read his file and I was aware he began to bite himself when he went in to care as a child. Self-harm was his oldest coping mechanism.

'Why did you pull out your stitches?' I asked pointing to the open wound on his leg.

'I'm protesting,' he replied, chewing on his own fat. 'Because I am in pain and no one is helping me.'

I explained his leg was hurting because he was putting a spoon into a wound. Pain was the body's defence mechanism against injury. A general rule of thumb was not to push past the pain barrier.

'I ate my thumb,' he said and showed me the stub where the distal phalanx was missing.

He wanted to have his dose of Tramadol increased. I explained he was on the maximum dose of 400mg in twenty four hours. It would be unsafe to go beyond it because he could damage his liver and kidneys. He could develop problems with his breathing and slip into a coma and die.

He extended his spoon towards me. The blood-stained fat wobbled on the spoon like a strawberry trifle.

'I'm a vegetarian,' I lied.

He shrugged and licked his spoon clean.

'The psychiatrists are coming in tomorrow Mr Mercury. You can discuss your medications with them, are you happy for me to put some fresh stitches in?' I asked.

'I can do my own stitches with a bit of metal and strips of blanket. It's getting more difficult because the scar tissue is tough. When I had MRSA the stitches fell out after two days. Maggots were crawling around in there. Then they turned into flies. I was their dad; The Lord of the Flies.'

Ginge's colleague suddenly heaved and was sick on the floor. The colour had drained from his face and he looked as if he was going to faint so I escorted him out of the cell for fresh air. Ginge covered the mess with toilet paper.

'I was in Helmand. Nothing fazes me Doc,' Ginge said when I asked if he was okay but I could see his face had become paler too. I needed to get the stitches in to Mr Mercury's wound so we could leave.

'It is probably best not to perform surgical procedures on yourself,' I said and took the spoon from him.

Vicky arrived with a surgical trolley and a suture pack.

'Will you be my glamorous assistant Vicky?' I asked.

'My pleasure Doc,' she replied in her sing-song voice.

I gloved up and assessed the ten cm wound on his leg. It was fetid and I breathed in and out through my mouth. Although Mr Mercury had eaten the fat he had not cut away the overlying skin and the wound edges had not curled and died. He was covered in scars and prison tattoos; wispy spiders, birds and fish appeared to flit in and out of his putrid wounds. Most of his tattoos were in blue ink as if he had doodled on himself with a heavy hand. There was a list of female names on his arm, presumably ex-girlfriends, because lines were crossed through them. On the knuckles of one hand he had marked 0121 and on the other BRUM so there was no mistaking he was from my hometown.

I anticipated that soon after I put in the stitches he was likely to open them up again and he would insert pens, spoons, dirt or faeces into the open sores. He had been prescribed protracted courses of antibiotics and was a case study in how to develop drug resistance. When he became septic he was transferred to hospital for intravenous antibiotics but the hospitals found him difficult to manage because he scared the other patients. He was abusive and swore at staff. He stole and swallowed jewellery, pens, batteries, spoons and whatever he could find and he had perforated his bowels on numerous occasions. The hospital doctors wrote angry letters to the prison about what a difficult patient he was. We responded defensively to ensure his care was not compromised by his abrasive personality.

He was banned from many of the local hospitals and he had to be taken to the edge of the county for emergency surgery. Sometimes he self-discharged himself and came back to the prison where he and his wounds festered.

Prison medicine occupied the grey zone between primary care, hospital care, mental health and substance misuse. It was often the place for people with nowhere else to go. The psychiatrists diagnosed Mr Freddie Mercury with an emotionally unstable personality disorder (EUPD). This was previously known as bipolar personality disorder and was not to be confused with a bipolar affective disorder. A personality disorder was not classified as a mental illness and he was not eligible to be sectioned under the Mental Health Act or to be transferred to a mental health unit.

Our thoughts, feelings and behaviour define our personality and Mr Freddie Mercury's personality caused longstanding problems for him and the people in his life. He had difficulty navigating his intense emotions which fluctuated faster than he could manage and he acted impulsively. He reported feeling numb apart from when he was self-harming and he had been suicidal for years. It was our job to keep him alive despite his daily efforts to kill himself. He took multiple overdoses and had tied ligatures around his neck many times. He was a hugely complicated gentleman and sometimes it felt as if we were prolonging his death rather than giving him a real life.

I took swabs of all his dirty wounds to send to microbiology to see if he was growing any unusual bugs and then I cleaned his sores with saline. As I brought the edges of the leg injury together I noticed the skin was overlaid with a huge Swastika tattoo.

'Well this is awkward,' I said.

He sighed loudly.

'The swastika is Indian,' I murmured and he pulled away from me, slightly.

'Why don't you go back to your country and look after your own people Doc?' Mr Mercury asked. His tone was not hostile. I had been asked this question before usually by old middle-class people. It seemed obvious to them that because I was brown I could not be English and must be from somewhere else. I had never felt anything other than British. Therefore my answer was rehearsed but heartfelt.

'You are my people,' I said.

His eyes flickered for a moment I thought we saw each other as humans and then I injected the edges of the gash with Lidocaine to make them comfortably numb. After a few minutes I prodded with the needle to see if the anaesthetic had worked.

'Does it hurt?'

He shook his head.

'Okay, I can start putting the stitches in. Are you ready?'

'I need to put my song on, it relaxes me, reminds me of the good old days when I used to get high.'

'Is it The Stranglers?' Ginge asked.

'No, it's Pass Out by Tinie Tempah,' Mr Mercury said, missing the joke.

'So you are not a fan of Queen?' I asked as he fiddled with his CD player.

'No, why would I be? I hate that queer. I just like the name.'

'Don't be nasty,' I admonished.

He shrugged. His song began to play and I had to hold on to his jumping leg. The singer's voice was whispery and confessional to start with as if Mr Tempah had awoken from a heavy night. Vikki and Ginge knew the words and began singing and dancing. I smiled at how ludicrous this entire situation was. I wondered what outsiders would think if they saw this? Sometimes it was hard to tell the prisoners from the staff other than the uniforms; we all became slightly unhinged from working in this peculiar environment.

I silently read a prayer before I put in the first stitch. I started in the middle of the wound and pulled the stitch through the tough scar tissue with some difficulty. Forward knots, back knots, forward knots, back knots and trying not to get them snagged on the forceps or his hair. When the song finished Mr Mercury played it again, and again, so the trance-like tune formed a trippy loop, forwards, backwards, forwards, backwards. I was staring down into a putrid wound and trying not to breathe in the stench. I was concentrating with such intensity the wound appeared to expand and contract before my dancing eyes. Mr Mercury was a known drug user and I wondered if he was exuding some noxious substance in his sweat and I was getting high?

'It is not the stitch that bothers me it is the skin and muscle being pulled back together that hurts. It must be quite satisfying fixing something that's broken?' he asked.

'It is,' I said with relief that it was over. I wiped away the blood and cleaned his leg. The swastika had not been distorted and I covered it in a dressing. Vicky and I counted the needles, thread, forceps and swabs to ensure we did not to leave anything behind that could be used in self-harm or as a weapon. He was already on antibiotics and the sutures could come out in five to seven days; if he did not take them out sooner. Vicky said she would assess him later. I implored him not to pull out the stitches I had worked so hard to place.

'You are alright Doc,' he said avoiding eye contact. It was the closest thing to a thank you. However difficult someone was I always tried to find something to like about them. I noticed his eyes were aquamarine with flecks of gold; like a tropical ocean in one of the images beside his bed. I felt a pang of sadness.

'You're welcome,' I said and I reached over and patted his clammy shoulder.

As I walked away to wash my hands I tried to comprehend what I had just witnessed.

'You're a brave man Doc,' Vicky said.

'How can we stop him harming himself?' I asked.

'They have tried everything to work with him over the years and nothing has worked. If you read his history you can see he has 'Shit Life Syndrome', he never stood a chance.'

I surveyed the chaos of the Inpatient unit. It was a long white corridor and had over a dozen cells on both sides. It reminded me of the scene from the film Silence of the Lambs where Agent Starling first met Hannibal Lector. The locked doors had a small observation panel at eye level and I was aware of being watched by unseen eyes. Many of the panels had been smashed and arms reached out through the broken glass. The din of screaming and banging doors was deafening. There was an overpowering smell of stale urine and faeces which indicated that some of the prisoners were on a dirty protest and either covering themselves or their environments in their own mess. Biohazard screens surrounded the doors because sometimes men on dirty protests targeted passers-by with squeezy bottles of their effluent. Some of the inpatients were sexually disinhibited and wanted to make eye contact as they pleasured themselves. It became second nature to duck as we passed by and keep our eyes on the filthy floor to avoid slipping and falling.

For me the strongest sense of a prison was the vibration felt in the bone marrow when a heavy gate was slammed shut. It took time to acclimatise and no longer jump or shudder when your bones rattled. Maybe this was what they meant when they said prison got in your bones? Once you were used to this environment it was difficult to leave. The thought of going back to community GP with a list of 'normal' patients filled me with dread. I liked not knowing what each day in a prison would bring. I thrived in the chaos.

'This is a very strange place,' I said.

'Oh yes,' Vicky laughed. 'Very strange people and that's just the staff.'

ASHA KRISHNA lives in Leicestershire and writes short stories and flash. She discovered homeschooling during lockdown but gave up as soon as her kids went back to school. She has been published in the Leicesterwrites anthology, Flash Fiction Festival anthology and 100 words of solitude. She enjoys running and travelling.

Asha's fiction draws on her experiences as an immigrant and she writes about contemporary Asian women walking a tightrope between tradition and modernity. She is also interested in exploring the lives of lesser known Asian historical characters through her stories.

My story 'Stepping into the world' took root during a family holiday to China. While travelling round the Chinese countryside, we stayed at a hotel run by two women who seem to work round the clock for their guests. They later told us that although they hosted visitors from all over the world, they had never travelled beyond their mountain town. It got me thinking about their backstory and what if they too dreamt of stepping into the world...

Asha was mentored by Rebecca Burns.

Stepping into the World

'The bank manager wants to see us this afternoon,' whispered Sheena when Anita picked up the phone, in the middle of checking a guest in.

'Yes, ok. Thanks,' hissed Anita as she put the phone back down and smiled at that man across the desk.

Anita tapped on the keyboard and slid the keys over to him. 'We hope you enjoy your stay.'

'Thanks.' Anita's eyes wandered over his muscular arms and strong shoulders when a tall leggy beauty behind him, stepped into view. She watched her tanned hands drain the last dregs from her water bottle.

Fixing her gaze on her, Anita said, 'There are cold water bottles in your room.'

The man smiled and was about to head to the stairs when he stopped. 'Are the limestone peaks really as magnificent as they say?'

'Many of our guests say that if you climb it once, you get addicted,' said Anita, smiling.

'Really?' His eyes seemed to bore into her, drawing her out.

'The peaks have been my playground as a child. I have done them all.' she said tilting her head a little.

'Great. In that case, we will find you as soon as we are ready.' He smiled, picking up his backpack and turning around towards the stairs with the woman following behind.

She watched their weary backs and battered backpacks. *Someday that will be me walking into a hotel, checking in…*

The hotel staff had often bumped into Anita daydreaming with her scrapbook open in front of her, filled with images of Big Ben, the Great Wall, and the Taj Mahal. They could almost see the strings of her thoughts travelling to these places. But they knew it was not easy being the daughter of their employer, the visionary who had transformed the town. Especially now that he was ailing. That day, they all had heard voices coming from her father's office after she had walked in…

And now every Friday Anita did the same thing on her day off. She would head over to the Karst peaks for an afternoon of adventure. As her fingers firmly gripped the crevices, before she could pull herself up, she would slowly move up to the giddying height till she got to the top. Once she got to the peak, with the wind gushing through her face and hair, she would find her place and pull out her scrapbook from the bag from the bag. As the pages fluttered in the breeze, it was as though the Big Ben and Great wall had escaped the confines of the pages, sprouting wings as they stepped into the bright sky. For that moment, it was her with those wings, drifting across the sky to destinations far away. And then as the light would slowly fade, she would make her way down the peak and climb back into the shell of her reality as she resigned herself to the week ahead.

The next day, Anita was just about to head to the dining room when Sheena called out. 'The manager wants to see us this afternoon.' Anita had her back to see so Sheena did not see the frown. She had been avoiding the bank manager, a man who had just moved into town and planned to settle down here after retirement. He had not been here part of the collective memory that had seen the family legacy take shape and it irked her. He was not there when the town was buckling under poverty and deprivation.

Stubborn Sharma, the townspeople had called him when they first heard he had bought the crumbling house on the hill. 'Five daughters, and instead of saving for their weddings, you are investing in rubble?' Their harsh tone was laced with concern.

But Sharma, who had returned after living in the city, still planned to invest in the tourist potential of the town. The Karst peaks drew rock climbing enthusiasts from all over the world and yet the town mostly depended on agriculture, which was getting more unpredictable each year.

Tourism would take the pressure off their unpredictable harvests, and although it felt like an uphill task, when the polished doors of their new hotel threw open its doors to customers, the whole town caved into his vision. Many failing businesses blossomed under the sunlight of its success. A tall statue now stood in the middle of town as their gratitude to the man who had transformed their fortunes.

Now, as she surveyed the room, she could feel her father's admonishing words when she spotted three chairs at a table. 'Never in threes, Unlucky.' She slid another chair to complete the set of four.

Her father lived and breathed the place thought Anita, every single thought directed towards cementing his vision with success.

Like the day when he bought the wooden carving and placed it at a vantage point in the hotel lobby. 'An artefact with history, the guests will love it,' he said and got a specially constructed alcove made with down lighters for maximum effect.

It was an exquisite piece, a wooden block chiselled in the shape of a karst peak mountain about fifteen inches high with a face peering out of it. A long flowing beard had been carved out with a nose and eyes that held a mesmerising gaze. The story like the carving itself had been polished so many times that it began to sound like family lore.

Every evening Sharma would join his guests in the dining room, serving nibbles of personal history along with their evening wine. The story was that during the post Indian independence era when the princely states had to hand over their titles and collections, his ancestor had managed it hide it away from the government. It had had been stealthily passed on from one generation to the next as a symbol of good luck and fortune.

The story improved with each retelling and soon Sharma began to believe in it too. The guests loved taking selfies with the heirloom that often made their way into holiday albums. A few, however, pushed for more. 'Is it for sale?' asked a collector one day.

Once a persistent guest had named an outrageous price. Their father topped up his glass with a regretful smile and asked Anita to come into his office later. 'Promise me, you will never let it go – the carving or the hotel,' her father said.

The guest however, had seen the gleam in Anita's eyes and quietly pressed a card into her hands. She had slipped it into their hotel expenses ledger, where it wedged down firmly between the pages.

'The hotel is not only my dream but also way of looking after you. You, as the eldest must understand that.' Sharma said.

And when their hotel celebrated their fifth anniversary, with a firmly established reputation and overflowing bookings, Sharma addressed the town.

'The hotel is not only my success it is yours too. I had to leave town because of no prospects. But now the world will come to us. We will never have to move away from our roots,' said their father, the smile of contentment brightening his face. But his words fell like a boulder blocking the mouth of the cave, crushing Anita's fledging dream under its weight.

Anita jolted out of her reverie when the phone rang. As soon as she picked up the phone, she recognised the voice. 'Can you and Sheena come down sooner?'

The bank manager carefully put down his coffee cup, as Anita and Sheena impatiently looked on. 'We have had another offer. They want us to strongly consider it.'

The office felt like a sauna with the door swinging open in the hope of fresh air. Anita bit her lip. 'We are not interested.'

'The accounts are not showing recovery. The hotel is still bleeding money,' said the manager, his bushy eyes narrowing through his spectacles.

'Our hotel has fabulous views and an established reputation. That is what they are after.'

'Yes. Which is why it is a particularly good offer. If not, they will wait until you sink. Which will happen if you do not fix the holes soon,' said the manager, his thick moustache catching the crumbs as he bit into a biscuit. 'If you agree to it, there will be a good size portion for all five of you.'

'But it was our father's dream, the most important landmark in the town...' said Anita looking at Sheena who was staring out of the window. Outside, a dog was running around in circles, trying to shake free of a tattered plastic bag caught around its ankles.

'The hotel's iconic landmark will remain, but under a different ownership, that's all. Your father was a good businessman. He would have agreed...' the manager stopped to sip his tea again

'The offer is open till the end of the month,' the manager said avoiding Anita's gaze. Sheena was still looking out of the window. The dog was gone but her gaze was still frozen.

That night in the reception lobby, Anita sat staring at the screenshot of the Taj on her computer, shining bright against the darkness of the room. The main chandelier lights had been switched off. Only the heirloom in the corner glowed with the down lighters on.

'Still awake?' Sheena stood at the door.

'Late check in. What are you doing here? You have to be in early for breakfast kitchen tomorrow.'

'I know. Been thinking about what the manager said.'

'Have you made a note of the special requirements for guests in Room No 302?' Anita asking despite knowing the answer.

'Yes. Vegan diet. All in hand.'

It was their father who had spotted Sheena's culinary abilities. 'She is good at picking the right flavours,' he had said.

'What if we took up the offer?' Sheena said voicing into the silence.

'Huh?'

'I mean then we can live our dream just like father did. I had already told him that I wanted to specialise as a baker. He agreed thinking I wanted to set up a bakery here. But I always wanted something of my own.'

Yet another fluttering dream getting crushed under the mammoth weight of their father's legacy. It never occurred to Anita that her sisters may have dreams of their own. Their father's real legacy lay in the fact that dreams could become real. But his grand vision was stifling other seedlings trying to take root. The wallpaper of the Taj Mahal was shining bright on her computer. By honouring his wife's death Shah Jahan had made her immortal. If the death of a dream gave life to new ones – it never perished but lived on forever.

Her gaze fell upon the heirloom in the corner. When the light shone on the rounded wooden face, it softened the features almost as if relaying a message.

'Hold on to it, the heirloom will see you through.' Her father had said.

Anita opened the ledger, flipping through the pages, until she got to the one with the business card in it.

KALBINDER KAUR was born in Stoke-on-Trent. She has had stories featured in several anthologies. As a writer-in-residence in 2017, she was lucky to work alongside Mind service-users to create poetry and short fiction. As well as working for a NHS mental health service, Kalbinder is currently completing a novel picking at a knot of Midlanders' lives and loves.

Lucky shares the story of a woman's affair with her brother's killer. A novel about sibling rivalry, a Midlands hometown and the ghost of a boy who didn't know how to stay dead. *Lucky* explores how to live after death. How to feel safe after damage.

I started working on Lucky after learning that a boy I'd grown up with had been stabbed to death in our Midland's hometown. What I've struggled with, writing 'Lucky' has been making sure that the titular character's story doesn't get squeezed out by the more obvious lines of enquiry. I want Lucky taking up the space she's entitled to, because behind every horrific headline involving an Asian man, there's a woman close-by with a hidden story, not just as a bit-player, but as a protagonist in her own right.

Kalbinder was mentored by Rod Duncan.

Lucky

Far, Far Away

Prologue
Stoke: Rest. In. Peace. Dolby

Everything's high, my eye picking out bright yellows in the night.

I can't be sure it's not just God – jealous that we're the light in the halo – everyone else in the dark tonight. But there's this solid shove from behind and I fall. My mates they try to pull me up. Christ they're weak. I'm no ten-ton man but they're all stupid with laughing.

A punch to his head floors Beanie. Gets up he does in a quick scuttle. Scuttle. Scuttle. They've stopped pulling me up. We've all stopped laughing.

There's this rapid fire rah-rah-rah getting louder and I focus, see a top-set so shiny I swear down they're glowing. It's the peek-a-boo of dog's teeth and straining mouth, his lead slack then pulled back tight by the angry guy's blonde.

My lads back away. Staggering first – then running – for the strength in numbers back at the party, just steps away from this fizzing anger. They race off through the quiet unbroken streets of night. Nights full of sleeping babies and snoring granddads, all at peace in the black centre of the halo.

And I'm left by myself on the foggy-up rim of this night. Not in the peaceful black and not in the glowing ring of love and hope where I had been. No. There's no strength in numbers for me.

I feel the cold of the pavement and get up now I've found meself. And I'm up telling them: come on then. Let's fucking do this. But must talk slow because I'm down again. My face on this lichen that's been making a life for itself in a crack between the wall and pavement. And I can see the frills of it, feel its beauty and the brightness of its yellow in the streetlight. All this time its supernatural yellow's been growing under my feet just to cheer me on. I try to get up, leave that lichen in peace but there's this weight on my eye. I feel the violence cracking my face open and their red streaks of anger spreading: it's too hot it just won't stop running

Stab's too blunt a word for the graceful sweep that makes me gasp. The dickhead's whistling blade jolts its shine into me again, trying to free my heart. But it's already free – don't those idiots know it? There's no need to scoop me out. I'm out already. Not dying but flying in the silence. Spinning in the black heart of the halo.

Chapter 1: Toronto

I pull the smoke past my lips deep into my throat, causing a splutter.

Rubbing my back as if I'm a colicky baby, Chrissy Gonzales offers to go in and get some water. I try again, drawing longer and deeper into the softness beyond the jagged edge at the back of my throat.

'Sorry,' I say, passing the joint back to Chrissy, 'I always get the roach wet.'

Chrissy draws gently on the roll-up as she looks out from her porch at the occasional passing halos of car headlights from the main street of Lake Shore.

'Dan's only just gone up to bed,' Chrissy tells me as though I've asked.

'Dan's a good man.' I say.

'Never picked a bad one yet.'

'You don't need to pick them, Chrissy. I always find that the bad ones pick you.'

'Ooh, Lucky girl. Now that sounds like the voice of experience.'

Safely tucked up in our chairs, we laugh now we're far from the worst of our mistakes.

'Ah. My reputation precedes me I see.'

'If only! You too English. Never thought we'd ever sit here so chill, let alone... Let alone this ...' Chrissy says, throwing her hands around to point at us sitting so cosy and smoking.

'This is so bad, isn't it? I'm going to lose some model wife points for this,' Chrissy says before laughing hard into the blanket, releasing a pig-like snort, making us both laugh harder.

Through the green buds of hydro she's pinched and rolled tonight, I feel myself re-written; becoming someone who laughs and lives easily. Feel myself moving out to Easter Island, far enough away for everything about my life to dissolve.

Chrissy holds our goodnight hug for so long, that I make it way past the uncomfortable stage, to simply collapsing on her. The longer she holds me, the more I feel my tiredness slither right out of me, abandoning me for the warmth of her T-shirt. By the time we part, my eyes are wide. Too awake, every hair on my arm stands on end for a fight. Me in this night, am just too bright to stay stuck, so count the seconds on the porch until Chrissy shuts her door. Then I sneak right back down my path again to walk past the identically bland houses that make up our orderly grid of sameness. Too bright to lie still, so wait on my porch until Chrissy shuts her door, then I sneak right back down my path again. Walk past the identically bland houses that make up our orderly grid of sameness.

Friends who knew me when I was married were surprised I'd ended up here. Reckoned it was a drunk-buy, as if my house was a mini-skirt or a feather boa that I'd picked up on the way home. Okay its true alcohol was involved. I'd been to a dive bar called the Zodiac with a girlfriend and wandered down the wrong street trying to get to the right bus stop. I near enough walked into the 'For Sale' post. And that was it. How I met the only home I ever owned. The only kitchen I've brought cabinets for, and bathroom I've attempted to tile.

Eager to keep the soaring feeling going, I turn onto the main street's stretch of run-down stores and the ever-glossy Shopper's Drug Mart. It's a failing neighbourhood friends tell me. Stubbornly unfashionable despite offering the ability to hop onto a streetcar that'll take you all the way to the delights of downtown. It's perfect, I think as I wander further down Lake Shore. And then I see it. The spark: The Zodiac.

The Zodiac remains open against all hope as better bars shut. Presumably staggering on due to die-hards drawn to the variety of pool tables.

I get a rye and coke, opposite a bar fly ready to swallow the lines that any guy vomits up. Good luck to her. I'm at the age where if I'm in a place like this, I'm here to drink not to meet the next Mr. Lucky. Only, it mustn't translate in my body language.

I don't know what he sees in my face that says I'm up for a chat but for the first time in years a guy at the bar asks if I'm having a goodnight. Am I? I can't tell. The music's too loud, each strum of the guitar strings breaking up the fogginess I'm trying to hold onto.

Offended by my silence, his friend says: 'You too good to talk to my pal?'

'I'm just not talking to anyone. It's not about goodness. There's a perfectly nice girl over there,' I say, in a voice that sounds distant and echoey, as if it's not mine.

'I bet you'd talk to him if he had a plate of tandoori chicken?'

'I am hungry.'

'Fucking, tandoori thighed bitch.'

Somewhere at a distance, there's a well-used synapse firing the mild shock he wants me to feel. But mostly I want that fucking tandoori chicken.

'Enough dude,' says the man who first approached me. 'She's not right.'

Once the men have headed off for the pool tables, the barman comes over.

'Sorry, I couldn't step in. He's a regular,' he shrugs.

'I don't suppose you have any tandoori chicken, do you?'

The barman seems to think I'm joking and goes back to wiping the glasses with a laugh.

The Zodiac's a mistake. Truth is it's never a good time but trying to keep your buzz going with dickheads all around is pretty much the worst. They're crashing my cloud.

If I knew what it was I'd carve it out, no lie. Why people think I might be interested? Makes the bar man think I have the headspace to give a crap. I should have left before the girl did. I definitely should have lied. Said I was a midwife instead of a nurse, before the guy could start spilling his guts to me across his wiped down bar. A big fuck-off mistake,

The Zodiac. I should have just bought a bottle and wandered home.

The bar man eventually crosses his slim tanned arms, cocks his head to the side. He's noticed my silence maybe? How engrossed I am in flicking the coaster? Either way he's leaving aside his mum's Parkinson's only to go onto the thing people always corner me about:

'So what's the most disturbing place you've been?'

The pink of his face is deepening. He's definitely hoping to get off on it.

In the past I've tried focusing on my ER-work instead of war zones, but it doesn't help. The question people really want to ask is how much damage I've witnessed. They're fascinated.

He wants something hideous, this tight spring of a guy. His TV-drama-hungry eyes need feeding. And feeding right now, just when I have nothing more to give.

I could stick it to him, say, 'Kids blown up by the mines their dads and granddads have planted to protect them.'

He wouldn't shudder at first then I'd build it up some more in the way folk like it:

'Imagine it, trying to clean up a limb, sew parts together, when it's just mush. And you've got all the family hysterics, while you try to work. The mother blacking out and crashing into your back as you're stitching mush-to-mush.'

He'd chew it over. Devour it.

As tired as I am, as tempting as it is to give him what he wants to make him go away I just can't do it. So muster the last of my Defcon-bitchface, and right before I walk to the door whisper, 'Without a doubt, the most disturbing place I've been is England and this bar, dickhead.'

The next time it doesn't feel like a dream, or a nightmare, I'm back in my wonkily tiled bathroom with my scratched coffee pot. I've obviously been multi-tasking. At least I have a pot to piss in.

That's when I hear Dolby:

You've been avoiding me sis. Clean your ears out. I said wake up you silly cow. Look I got to tell you something.

I open my eyes. But he's not here. Not in my home, just in my head. Yet I smell the wood smoke and clove of his birthday aftershave. But no, it's just a voice, like he used to be when he first died all those years ago.

Just listen like you used to, Lucks.

'Dolby?'

Who else is it going to be? How many dead brothers you got, lass?

'I can smell you. Come closer.' But Dolby being Dolby, just carries on talking about himself.

Forget Pi. Bully boy can look after hisself. Forget him. Go for me. Go back find Ali. My life was always meant to be a romance. Find my Alison.

I don't bother saying his name again. I know he's gone.

Fuck. He's come so far from home just to find me. May as well just give up now.

'What do I get, Dolby? Dolby?' I shout to the empty bathroom. Typical of baby brothers, coming and going when it suits them.

Will he leave me be if I do it and find Ali? How would I even start? Trust Dolby to find me again after so long. Crossing the Atlantic to find me. Vindictive sod. And already ordering me around.

Even though you know it's bad. It'll undo you. Sometimes you just have to say fuck it. No matter that Pi's unpredictable. Dolby's a head-fuck. Sometimes you say yes. Or I say yes, at least. Because I'm tired. Because I just can't stand to wait for the worst any longer. The worst keeps finding me anyhow.

Less than 24-hours later I'm on the plane back to the English Midlands. Back to my homeland and the dregs.

Chapter 2: Homesick

I can't say if Birmingham International's that much different since my flight out to Toronto all those years ago. Too many airports in between. Too much time standing in lines for tetchy border officials. I've no right to expect a welcoming party. In truth, I don't think Rupee counts as one.

Sharp eyes, tight mouth ready to spring open and chew you up. She's a bolder, older, trimmer version of the woman my big bro Pi married. I'm a teenager again on the sight of her: my stomach drops, mouth dries. Front-footed, Rupee quickly traps me in a hug that makes me long for the scuffed sterility of Arrivals.

For a second, there's a shadow in the corner of my eye. I turn jittery, but it's just someone's luggage trolley.

'You didn't have to collect me. I would've found my way,' I say.

'Lucky! My God, look at you!' Rupee fluffs my hair. She was married to my brother, the last time she did that. Surely she doesn't get to do that now? But of course, I let her.

'Hi Rupee-bhabi.'

'I think it's time you dropped the bhabi.'

We smile at each other, divorcee-to-divorcee.

What she's noticing? There are the three wiry white hairs that sometimes fall on my face, re-appearing despite me tearing them out by the roots. The odd mouth-to-nose lines I blamed on the year I'd smoked in my 20s, in rebellion at being a wife. I suddenly feel every one of my thirty-six sneak up on me. No instalments, Rupee's getting just one giant gulp. And boy how she's drinking it up.

'You travel light,' she says tapping on my wheelie suitcase. 'Or it that you not expecting to stay, Lucks?'

I try to laugh it off, while she crosses her arms and stares at me hard searching for the answer.

Truth is I don't know myself.

'Rupee, why can we never talk like sisters? You know I always thought of you as one.'

She smiles and grips my shoulders with both hands. 'I have sisters. This is how they talk. Now get in the car, before you change your mind.'

The old country has shrunk. Houses, roads, cars, trees, and people are all squashed up as if we really are on a tiny island where if we breathe in too deeply, our bellies will topple the people on the edge into the sea. I feel sick. The cloying spice isn't helping.

Don't whinge, I tell myself. The return's gentler than I could have hoped for. The route south of the airport to the Arden village where Rupee now lives is new, freeing me from remembering what had stood where and dwelling on who I'd been when I'd last seen it.

Choose me not him.

I fucked up. But Pi pushed me to it. Cost me the best girl in Stoke in all.

Man it hurts even now – how I tried to hold Ali's hand only for it to snake away.

Go away. Not now Dolby, I can't deal with you here. Get out.

I wipe my face. And once again dab at my forehead with my tissue. But still, I can feel my brother's return. It's as fine as spider thread lying on my skin. But it's there. So it's not just the hydro. He's really back.

Rupee chats about her kids in between muttering about the other drivers.

'They would have liked to have been here to meet you, Lucky.'

'I'm surprised they still remember who I am.'

I try to draw on the comfortable generic English-Canadian differences of scale. But Rupee won't shut up.

'You're their Lucky bhoua. *Of course* they do. You're still their blood.'

It's a long time since I thought of them in those terms. Our history too short and long ago. Technically we share DNA, but it's too late to be any type of aunt to them now, even If I wanted to be.

'Your niece is back in September in time for the new term, so you might even catch up, if you decide to stay.'

I won't take the bait. I move to her other child. 'And your son, he's still out in Oz?'

'He's made a life there. I'm a grandma now. Can you believe it?'

And I can. The family tree always ran through Pi as the eldest. It felt right that him, and his wife – ex-wife – should preside over grandkids and great-grandkids. While me and

105

Dolby's dead branches would hollow and fall. After all Pi is short for Piara. Beloved. And boy did me and Dolby know it.

Dolby. Did he really want me to find Alison?

Bloody brothers. They'll be the death of me.

I cough the gloop of rising acid from my throat into a tissue. Tuck it back into my sleeve to hide my grossness, my fear under the creased cotton.

No, I can't handle it right now. I just can't. It's safer to limit myself to a tourist mind-set than memory lane so I try to drink in the foreignness of the dual carriageways and the farmland on its fringes. The carriageway starts to narrow into a country lane, winding over humpback-bridges, past lone cottages and boarded-up pubs, entering and leaving swells of villages and new-builds patch-worked between the fields and business parks, until we turn opposite a church and triplet of cottages and Rupee says, 'This one's ours.'

The driveway seems much too small for such a grand house. I wonder if Rupee's neighbours know that before she was the queen of the manor, she lived in a flat above the family's BrightDay Convenience Store.

Now she's home, Rupee transforms into someone softer, lighter. A perfect hostess leading me with easy smiles through the large hallway, passing doorways leading into an elegantly furnished sitting-room on one side and a suitably austere study on the other. It's far from the cluttered, fusty home she had with my brother. I shiver. Where the hell does Pi even live now? I realise I never thought to ask.

There's only one photo of her new man, but there are signs of him in the hallway with its wax jacket and fishing rod. Rupee the most desi old-school of girls has replaced my brother for a country squire. I've seen it all now.

In my years as a Canadian it's exactly this view out of Rupee's kitchen that has displaced the tarmac and concrete of England as I knew it. Once when a manager had returned from vacation with pictures of herself in shorts and walking boots stalking through the Lake District with a copy of Peter Rabbit against her cheek, embarrassingly I'd found myself sighing at some imaginary England, adopted stanza by stanza from school but only ever glimpsed from motorways and trains.

Now here it is for real, through the windows and open patio doors. Here it is now I'm a visitor – all laid out: mild hills and woodland, rising and falling around the back of the house, tucking the garden into the hillside. An English backdrop fit for postcard-memories and fantasy homelands. And out of us all it was Rupee who found it.

I feel faint. Black splodges and white stars are blotting out the landscape. I grab for a seat before I can fall. It's too much. This is exactly why I shouldn't have come: number five on my con list: all journeys end with the disappointment of meeting myself on arrival. Never anybody smarter or braver, just little Lucky Bassi.

'That's right, sit down,' says Rupee. 'I'll get some water.'

I'm no good outside my rut.

Rupee holds onto my shoulder, tight and scared.

'You don't have to prop me up. I'm okay.'

'You sure?'

It's her guilt talking. Why did she bring me back?

'It's just low blood pressure. Give me a minute.'

I take a second to walk back through the house to the front window where I look over the road to the cottages on the other side. The tightness relaxes and the burning in my chest lifts. I imagine myself out of this idyll into a Midlands I'm more familiar with and begin to walk around the cluttered dark rooms across the road instead. I am now. I am now.

I am now. What kind of bullshit is that?